A Soul's Journey Home

Returning to Love

Angela Bushman

A Soul's Journey Home

Returning to Love

Shine Your Light
Kailua, Hawaii

Published by: Shine Your Light
111 Hekili Street, Suite A498
Kailua, Hawaii 96734 U.S.A.
www.shine-your-light.com

Library of Congress Control Number: 2012953227

ISBN 978-0-9884334-0-3

Edited by Jason Robertson

Cover Design by Amy O'Donnell

First edition

Printed in the United States of America

CONTENTS

This book is dedicated to all the beautiful souls who assisted me on my journey to self-awareness: my children, former husband, family, friends, strangers, and spiritual teachers. Each of you played an important role, from nurturing me to challenging me, in order that I may have the opportunity to experience, learn, expand and ultimately, return home to love.

ACKNOWLEDGMENTS

I am extremely grateful to the special angels that appeared in my life at just the right time to inspire, encourage, support, nurture and prod me on, each in their unique way. Mary Higley and Jeanne Staron stood beside me as soul sisters, forever believed in me and helped even the most difficult of transitions, both physical and emotional, to be interesting and bearable experiences. Ron Guerrero, Ed Ho, and Carter Black supported me with their friendship, creative energy, gentle hearts, meals and countless rides to the airport.

My mother and father helped me understand that I could do anything that I could dream. My children gave me their unconditional love and support. An abundance of teachers and healers shared their unique message and support to help guide my journey. The dance communities of Phoenix, Oahu, San Diego and Sydney, Australia opened their loving arms to me and made me part of their family. Glenn Poulain led me on my first photo shoot, and was responsible for my photo on the back cover. Many other friends, too numerous to name, shared their wisdom and support with me in ways that I will never forget.

Last but not least, my gratitude goes to Light Books Publishing, specifically Dr. Zeal Okogeri, who showed up in my life the minute that I said I was ready to write, and quickly helped me to understand the amazing process of turning words into a book. I thank all of you for being the bright lights in my world.

INTRODUCTION

This is a story of transformation. It is the story of my journey from a fragmented soul to a happy, healthy, and complete person. It is about how I found the pieces of myself that I had denied throughout my life.

My journey is all encompassing, exploring the physical, mental, and spiritual aspects of myself. This journey has led me to many teachers, cultures, and experiences around the world. Ultimately, the journey itself was the catalyst for my transformation: the discovery of who I am and what I am on earth to do. It allowed me to step out of a self-imposed box and give myself the freedom to create the life that I want to live, and thereby to find peace and contentment.

You don't need to come from any particular spiritual background to understand this book. You don't even need to believe in anything sacred. This book doesn't speak to any particular religion, culture, race, or gender. I speak to you as an individual beyond the confines of religious philosophy. We are all human, and life's journey, while unique to each individual, is the same on the grand scale.

As you follow my story, emotions may arise. Observe and embrace these feelings. It takes courage and trust to go against the flow, to break patterns that have become ingrained over a lifetime. In preparation, you might want to have some tissues on hand and to be ready for your heart to sing. Nothing else is necessary, apart from an open mind willing to experience everything you feel.

Everyone has the power to be true to him or herself, but I believe that at some point we all give our power away. No one takes your power from you. Rather, we give our power away by feeling that we do not have the ability to create what we want, to be ourselves and to live our truths. We give our power away when we try to fit into the stereotypical mold of societal values or to be what others want us to be.

This book will help you to expand your mind and to notice occasions in the past when you gave your power away. By leading you to the realization that you are responsible for creating everything in your life, this book will also help you to find a place of contentment and balance that most people have always desired.

My journey will show you the theory in action, and the emotions felt along the path to self-discovery and empowerment.

By seeing the steps that I chose to find peace, it is my hope that you will likewise be inspired to take action and to embrace the life you have always wanted to live. So here is my story from the heart. Do with it what you will. My hope is that it will bring you the peace and inspiration to embrace your true identity as soul.

Shine Your Light

One

Freedom

FREEDOM IS SOMETHING THAT YOU GIVE YOURSELF
AND NO ONE ELSE CAN EVER TAKE AWAY.

—JOURNAL ENTRY, 2011

Not long ago I sat in one of my favorite places in the world, a place where the ocean meets the land, the sun shines brightly, and the wind cradles me in its arms. This inspirational place, on Kailua Beach in Hawaii, is a place I now visit frequently. Near my new home on Oahu, it is a place of peace, beauty, grace, freedom, and contentment. It is a physical representation of where I am mentally and spiritually.

As I sat in this magical place, I felt my rhythm start to blend into the rhythm of the wind, the waves, and the bird song. It was a typical day at Kailua beach, with people from all over the world relaxing on the warm white sand, riding the gentle waves on their boogie boards, and making sand castles not far from me.

As I let go and melted into the flow of energy around me, I started to hear words very clearly in my mind. With only my cell phone on hand, I tapped the words onto the little keypad as fast as I could, tears of joy flowing down my face the whole time. I felt something powerful was happening to me, and I was grateful to be able to record it for deeper understanding and reconnection later.

By the time I had finished typing, energy was gushing though my body, like water bursting through a dam that had just ruptured. My chest throbbing, I felt like I was gasping for air. Apart from my own place of peace, I had no idea where I was physically; neither did I know what time it was, nor where I stopped and everything else began.

I was unaware of anyone around me. If someone was witnessing this deeply personal moment, it didn't matter to me. I knew that everything was as it should be, and if others were observing what I was going through, it was because they should somehow be a part of it.

It was a pinnacle moment for me, a realization that I was "there," whatever that meant. It was a wonderful gift that I was finally able to give to myself. All the hard work, the challenges, the adjustments, and the growing pains had been worthwhile.

The words that came through me that day became the poem and the rhythm for my way of embracing life. As I reread the words, I realized that others might also use them as a tool for their own self-liberation. This revelation led me to where I am today: an Intuitive Empowerment Coach helping others to embrace their true soul.

Read the affirmations below carefully. As you do, observe which messages you read effortlessly, and which cause resistance. Retain this awareness as you venture on through the book. See what speaks to you, as you learn what spoke to me.

I Give Myself Freedom…

1. … to smile when I feel like it.
2. … to choose what is right for me.
3. … to be happy because I want to be.
4. … to cry when sadness starts to rise, and to give thanks for the lesson learned, but to not hang onto the sadness or to let it have power over me.
5. … to value and walk in my truth and to understand that my truth is not the same as others' truth.
6. … to see that every day is a gift to choose how to experience life in this physical world.
7. .. to learn, to grow, and to expand without judging myself or others.
8. … to be free of others' opinions of me, as I know that

everyone has their own unique perspective on reality.

9. ... to allow others to be precisely where they are on their journey and to know that it is not my responsibility or right to change anyone but myself.

10. .. to trust that I can take care of myself and keep myself safe.

11. .. to love myself unconditionally.

12. .. to choose without regret.

13. .. to love and to be loved.

14. .. to create healthy boundaries for myself.

15. .. to make decisions free of guilt, knowing that I will choose what is for the highest good whether or not others understand.

16. .. to give without the expectation of anything in return.

17. .. to accept what is given to me, knowing that I am worthy to receive abundance.

18. .. to enter into relationships with others, while keeping my individuality.

19. .. to see the beauty in everyone, even when they cannot.

20. .. to know that everyone is a unique part of the whole.

21. .. to understand how powerful I am, to stand in my power, and to not be afraid of it.

22. .. to understand that I am creating my life experiences.

23. .. to see hard times as opportunities to grow, and to find strength I would otherwise not have known.

24. .. to not repeat lessons already learned.

25. .. to be real, to express my passions in my own unique way, and to speak my voice when I choose.
26. .. to be brave enough to be a pioneer on frontiers where others have not attempted to go.
27. .. I give myself freedom to be myself and to shine my light.

Now that you see where I am, know that I have not always been an Intuitive Empowerment Coach. In fact, I had a much different life before I went through my personal transformation. The story of my old life is not uncommon today, though the way I grew beyond it is.

One of the greatest lessons I have learned is that each of us has to choose to be courageous enough to take the journey. No one else can start you down your path. The fact that this book is now in your hands is the first sign you are ready to be lead further along your journey. I hope to help you create a loving space for continuing on your path.

As you read about the beginning of my journey in the next chapter, remember that each person's journey towards self-revelation is unique. You should not follow me, but rather follow your inner self. It is when each individual finds his or her true self that they can genuinely begin to contribute back to the wholeness of which we are all a part.

Shine Your Light

Two

The Tunnel

THE TUNNEL IS A TIME OF TRANSFORMATION,
A RE-BIRTHING OF ONE'S SELF.

—JOURNAL ENTRY, 2005

I call it, "Being in the tunnel. "This is where you are when you are not what you used to be, and at the same time, have not yet become what you will be. It feels like there is no light, no way out, except to move forward. There is no view, and the sides feel tight around you. It is a dark place where there seems to be no one else but you. The only voice you hear is yours. It is the place where you start to find all of the pieces that are you. The pieces that have lived in the dark and the ones you have hidden from yourself all along. The tunnel is a time of transformation, a re-birthing of one's self."

—Journal Entry, 2005

My journal is finally finding a use. The previous entry is one that I recently dug out of a crate of my writings that I've been carrying around for years. Written in my early forties—the period that began my transformation—it describes a time in my life that others commonly refer to as "the dark night of the soul."

I continually referred to this time as being "in the tunnel." It felt like I was walking down a closed-in hallway, leaving behind one part of my life and heading toward the next. I did not know where I was going. I just knew I had to keep walking, one step at a time, even though it was dark and scary. I was by myself on the path, and it was an inward journey to places I had never been. Sometimes it felt as if I was Alice in Wonderland falling down the rabbit hole.

I was married and a mother of three healthy and wonderful children—two girls and a boy. Since the birth of my first child fifteen years earlier, I had been a stay-at-home mom. As I look back on my incredible journey, I now recognize how blessed I was to be an integral part of my children's early lives.

After putting myself through college, I married my high school sweetheart. Together, we found good jobs, moved several times for career growth, and finally settled in Scottsdale, Arizona. Our diligent work had finally started to pay off and we were beginning to live quite a comfortable lifestyle. We were living the traditional dream of most modern families.

But under the surface, things were beginning to fray. Although I had never had a problem sleeping, I suddenly found myself waking up for no reason in the middle of the night with a racing mind. During the day, I was becoming anxious and feeling less and less connected with the daily routine that had been such a comfortable part of my life. Something wasn't right and I couldn't quite put my finger on it.

I remember the day I woke up and the world seemed to be crashing in all around me. My whole body started to shake, my breath quickened, and I felt close to fainting. I called my husband at work. "Are you okay?" he asked. "No, I am not," I told him. I was frozen in fear and did not know what was happening to me.

I don't remember what happened after I hung up the phone. I only remember being stopped in the tracks of my daily routine, and gripped by a fear that held my total attention. "Stop walking away from it," something was saying to me. "It is time to see what you need to see."

"What is going on with me?" I asked myself. I had worked hard and created a seemingly wonderful life and yet "things" just didn't feel right.

I realize now that part of the anxiety was a feeling of disconnection from my husband. Although he had always been very dedicated to his job, it seemed that work had completely absorbed him in the last couple years and I was missing having a partner in my life. His long-term goal was to work hard enough to retire early. When we had moved to Arizona two years before, he had told me he needed to prove himself at work and I had said that I understood. While he focused on his career, I dove into a life of connecting to our new community on my own, and spent most of my time focused on the lives of our children.

From where I stand now, I realize what an unhealthy imbalance we had created for ourselves and for our children. This happens to so many families: getting caught up in the rat race of the Western world. While focusing on what the world said was important, we forgot to value our personal relationships. We spent all of our time working to accumulate things, filling our shelves with superficial objects, while our human connections lay neglected in the dark corners of our lives. Worst of all, we spent most of our time living for the future, completely ignoring the present.

At the time, I did not understand these problems. I just tried to be a supportive spouse and mother, and to help everyone else to become the best they could. I did not question any of it. I just went with the flow of what our culture says is the path to happiness: to "have it all," whatever that means.

During this time I kept asking myself, "Where have I gone?" And "Where am I?" It seemed I wasn't even a part of the equation anymore. When had I given up so much of myself? Somewhere in the course of my journey, I had lost the "me" in my marriage, in my family, and in every aspect of my life.

I had not always been a stay-at-home mom. Although one of my loves was psychology, I ended up studying accounting in college, probably because it seemed like a more practical route. After graduating, I passed my Certified Public Accountant exam and worked for a large auditing firm in Dallas and then with another firm in Kansas City as an internal auditor.

As long as I could remember, I had dreamed of having a career in which I could enjoy the use of my analytical and problem-solving skills. I was always an excellent student and craved to learn, to explore, to help, and to fix. Now I understand that I had strongly developed my masculine energy—my analytical side—or what some people consider left-brain activity.

After a few years in the work force, the thrill of motherhood took me by surprise when I became pregnant with my first child. Being a very bad delegator at the time, I left my job to take care of my newborn daughter. Raising our child seemed to me to be the most important job in the world, and I wanted to be fully in charge of guiding this amazing little being.

A Soul's Journey Home

I had no idea that full-time motherhood would teach me as much, if not more, than I taught my child. It was the natural next step in my life's curriculum, providing yet another building block for use in my life's work down the road. Motherhood developed my feminine side—my nurturing and creative side—or what some people call right-brain activity.

But this understanding all came later. Let's return to the tunnel.

The friction with my husband escalated during this time that most people would call a "mid-life crisis." Frustrated, my husband told me that I used to be strong and that now I wasn't. One night he actually yelled, "You need to find your passion," as he struggled to deal with the transformation I was going through.

Although I did not appreciate his lack of compassion, I now clearly recognize that he had delivered exactly the truth I needed to hear. It was just not necessary to be confronted so aggressively.

It was true: I needed to find my passion. As I later learned, finding my passion would allow me to find myself. Everyone else's passions had become my priority, while my own were so neglected that I did not even remember what they were. Of course, being a wife and a mother was amazingly fulfilling, but I had given up my core self in the process. Without my true self, I could not fully contribute to my family or to anyone else. With this realization, I started to fall into depression.

As I continued journeying through the tunnel, emotions arose that spoke to me so clearly. Pieces of me popped up looking to be reclaimed, and I began to converse with them, learning something each and every time. I began to embrace the journey even though I was afraid of what I might find.

The universe finally had my full attention and I was open to seeing what I had not seen before. Sometimes we have to be brought to our knees before we say "Uncle," as the saying goes. The shadows of myself that I had hidden from were starting to present themselves in different ways.

Sometimes I would read just the right book at just the right time and the information would simply strike me. It would hit home and resonate with me so deeply that I knew it was my truth. At other times I would see a certain behavior in others and realize that I, too, owned that behavior.

Because I was suddenly open to receiving this information, the universe began to send it at me in full force. I have to admit that sometimes it stung and sometimes it made me cringe, but it was time to be brave enough to accept whatever would help me to heal.

I started to become aware of my control issues. As I observed my everyday behavior, I realized I was trying to control everyone's emotions. I do not like friction and, of course, wanted my family to be happy. Sometimes I didn't want to see someone else struggle or be in pain, and at other times I simply did not want to rock the boat and cause those emotions myself. I thought it was good to protect others from pain. I had not realized that I was blocking other's lessons when I did this. Who was I to interfere with their growth, thinking I knew what was best for them? I felt responsible for everyone's happiness and did not understand that they had to find it in their own way and in their own time.

Lack of expression was another dark shadow that I had not seen before. It was my fear of speaking up about what I believed was right. Somehow I had lost my voice by softening it too much over the last ten years. My feminine side had become so strong that I had become more of a listener and receiver than a person with a voice and an opinion. I found that I had become too timid when stating my wants, needs, and opinions. And when I did, it seemed that they were not respected or valued. It occurred to me that if I did not value my own opinions or beliefs, then why would anyone else?

My fear of vulnerability also presented itself. I found that I could easily see and address someone else's vulnerability, but was afraid to show the world mine. Why was I unable to expose myself, even within my intimate relationships? Why did my heart have to be so protected? How did I expect to have a close intimate connection if I was afraid to be open with someone else? And how was it that I could be in a relationship for so long and still not be vulnerable in it?

The more I thought about it, the more it dawned on me that all these shadows emerging in the tunnel stemmed from the same issue: the overall lack of value I had for myself. I started to realize that I valued other people in my life far more than I valued my own needs, wants, and priorities. Failing to value myself certainly wasn't good for me, and it definitely wasn't something I wanted to pass on to my children as their role model.

While in the tunnel, my family visited the Big Island of Hawaii one summer for a week's stay at a quiet resort on a gorgeous beach. It is common for those who can afford it to get out of the 110 degree Arizona heat to seek refuge on the beautiful shores of Hawaii or California.

My visit to the Big Island magnified all the feelings I was having at that time. Lounging in the sand with an active volcano watching over me, I could feel the change bubbling up throughout my body. It felt as though my inner volcano was about to erupt.

As I sometimes do when I travel, I brought a rock from the island home with me. I know you leave behind a part of your energy when you visit a new place, and in exchange I wanted to take a piece of Hawaii's energy home. At the time, I wasn't aware of the legendary curse of Pele, the powerful volcanic goddess. Pele forbids anyone from taking away a piece of volcanic rock, the life force of the islands. It is said that simply visiting the Big Island of Hawaii can release emotions that lie below the surface of your life. But to take a rock off the island is to have the power of Pele transform your life at an unimaginable rate and force. I was about to learn this first hand, as major transformations awaited me at home.

I felt fear as I realized my world was about to change. I knew it would be a struggle because I would try to hold on to what I knew. But there comes a time when holding onto something that has already served its purpose becomes more damaging than beneficial. It is hard to let go, because we only know how to respond from how we have responded in the past. To learn to respond and decide to act differently requires us to step beyond the threshold of fear.

Shine Your Light

Three

The Light

I AM A NURTURER, A SEER, A CLOWN, AND A FLOWER.
—JOURNAL ENTRY, 2006

My journey through the tunnel towards a new me had begun. My mission now was to find out more about who I was. The more I looked, the more I realized there are a variety of systems for this type of self-exploration. I had shown my interest and was open to receiving, and now it seemed that everywhere I turned I was lead to more information. It was no coincidence that all the information pointed in the same direction.

I discovered some of the first good material at the library. At one point, I spent many hours at our local library while my son attended his after-school reading lesson. Three times a week for an hour or more, I would peruse the shelves, exploring subjects I had never before encountered. I understand now that we design our life so that the universe may lead us to our information.

At that time, the library was my teacher and the voice of the universe.

Numerology was one of the first subjects that spoke to me, and I loaded up on books to take home. After the kids went to bed, I would read voraciously until the early hours of the morning. Numbers spoke to my analytical side and I enjoyed exploring the ancient numerological systems that are reputed to be road maps of life. Numbers can point you toward the paths, lessons, and personalities you will encounter while on this physical plane of existence. Numbers can be powerful guideposts for those open to receiving their information.

I specifically remember sitting in my bedroom one evening, reading a book about numerology. As I saw my true soul presented to me in the numbers that lay before me, a feeling that is hard to explain overcame me. It was as if I had found an old friend whom I had not seen in lifetimes. More than that, it was as if someone finally knew me and could describe me better than anyone ever had in my life. This moment touched my heart so deeply that tears of joy ran down my face as I sat immersed in the knowledge resonating with my own truth. In that moment, I began to truly understand the feeling of finding something that resonates with truth.

As I came to understand the language of numerology, I

learned that my life path number is eleven. Eleven represents the life path of a spiritual messenger. Those on the path of eleven must learn to be independent in relationships. I soon found out how strong these themes would become as I started to align with my authentic life path.

Continuing to explore numerology, I saw that I am on earth to deliver a message, to be a bridge between the conscious and unconscious realms. However, the underlying message was that I must first complete my personal, inner work before I could step into my role as a channel. This rang true to my soul, yet I didn't fully understand the process needed to complete this transformation. Though I had no details or framework for what was to come, I was beginning to trust this interconnected knowledge base system that I was starting to consciously connect with, which I started to refer to as Spirit, or sometimes, the Universe. So I stayed open to the information that was coming to me, and kept moving forward on my journey.

During this time, I remember frequently having a question or an upsetting situation on my mind, when suddenly a song would come on the radio that directly spoke the message I needed to hear in that moment. Other times, I would run into a friend and during casual conversation, the answers to my unspoken questions would present themselves. I was starting to witness coincidences everywhere, and was learning to follow my instincts, wherever they lead.

One afternoon I was driving down the street listening to the radio. An astrologer came on the air, and without even thinking about it, I pulled over to the side of the road and wrote down her phone number. I had never had an astrological reading before, and have to admit that I felt bubbly excitement combined with a slight fear at the possibility. I knew I was being lead to someone who could expose my deepest makeup, but was I ready to receive more information from Spirit? It was one thing to receive messages from a book, but another thing entirely to have a stranger probe my inner workings. In spite of my apprehension, I called her to set up an appointment. As I drove to her house, I continued to wonder what she might reveal to me and whether she would trigger further shifts in my world.

When I arrived, I waited patiently in a small garden until she finished her previous session. I tried to soothe myself with the melody of the wind chimes and the playfulness of the whimsical garden, but instead found my heart starting to race. I now realize I knew I was about to reconnect to parts of myself that I had suppressed for far too long. I felt vulnerable knowing a complete stranger was going to witness my hidden truths and say them out loud. I felt I would be held more responsible when another human knew my soul's design and could see the lessons I needed to work on to return to my path.

Once inside, we sat across from each other at her desk, just off from her living room. She was quiet and focused, and showed no signs of wanting to comfort me as I sat shaking in her presence.

She pulled up my chart on her computer and started to share bits of information with me. I didn't understand some of it, and I told her that I did not even know what made me pull my car over and write down her number. She just looked at me. Actually, it was more of a glare. Then she showed some books to me and suggested that I read them, seeing that I did not yet grasp who I was and what I was here to do. "Do you remember any of this?" she asked as she showed me books on the mark of Yod, crop circles, UFOs, channeling, astrology, and more.

Though none of this made sense to me at the time, I now understand that everything happens for a reason. Sometimes, when we are stuck in a closed room, the doors open for us in unexpected ways. Or else seeds of information are given to us that will begin to sprout later, when we least expect it.

I went looking for a few of the books the astrologer had recommended. It felt strange hanging out in the metaphysical area of the bookstore. I think it was because I was approaching those topics from the view of mainstream society, and I had absorbed some of the material prejudices of the modern world. Now that I have had a chance to travel and explore other cultures, I often wonder why so many in the Western world disapprove of ancient wisdom that other cultures cherish and practice openly. Is it because they are afraid of what they might learn about themselves and the world they have created? Or is it because some cultures and organizations have labeled these ancient systems as evil, out of fear of the personal power they could bring individuals?

As I dove into astrology, the amount of information seemed endless. I was amazed by the deep insights that continued to resonate with me. Not only did astrology resonate with me, but it also validated the information I had gathered from numerology.

Astrology became my new passion, and I found my chart was that of the "wounded healer." My chart clearly showed that I would first have to figure out how to heal myself before I could teach the process to others. It seemed I was destined to be my first client! Experimenting with myself, I expanded my knowledge of this esoteric information.

Astrology taught me what various celestial bodies represent to humans, and how the position of the planets at our time of birth can show us the blueprint of our being. I was most intrigued by the North Node and Chiron, two lesser-known relationships, often not considered in everyday astrology readings.

The position of the North Node of the Moon within an

astrology chart reveals a person's major life lessons. Chiron's location in an astrological chart identifies a person's deepest wound. In fact, the asteroid Chiron is referred to as "the wounded healer." I found this to be a powerful guide in shifting my perspective on the painful challenges that do not hinder, but in fact facilitate personal transformation, growth, and ultimately, self-empowerment.

If you're interested in learning more, I found the book *Astrology for the Soul* to provide extensive information on the lessons involved in each placement of the North Node. The book, *Chiron: Healing Body & Soul* helped me to identify my specific wounds and the gifts that they could provide to help me grow. You'll find the author and publisher's information about these and other books in my cited sources at the back of this book.

I then studied the meaning of a Yod, which is a unique relationship between multiple points on an astrological chart. A Yod is often referred to as the "Hand of God." Though very difficult to interpret precisely, it represents a particularly strong combination of challenges within a chart, which if overcome, create tremendous opportunities for growth. As I have a Yod in my chart, I would have this opportunity for tremendous growth if I could navigate my set of simultaneous lessons.

I was amazed at the consistency of the information I was given by two very different systems of knowledge. Just as numerology had, my astrological chart showed that after I had completed my inner development, I would be a bridge between the realms. I was destined to bring spiritual information into the physical world. I would do so with my gifts of verbal and written communication, combined with my highly sensitive nature.

My sensitive nature was something else I started to understand. Up to this point, it had seemed like a weakness. My husband had told me more than once that I was too sensitive, and that it wasn't normal. I now realize that sometimes your strengths and gifts can be your weaknesses until you understand what they are and how to use them wisely. Sometimes the parts that make us unique are what we shut down in an attempt to fit in and not be different. Noticing my high sensitivity presented to me again and again by various sources, I returned to the library to see what I could discover.

I soon found books addressing the "highly sensitive" soul. The books explained how some people have a much higher sensitivity than others. Until they learn how to understand and manage their inherent nature, these highly sensitive souls may face unique challenges foreign to other people. Highly sensitive souls, sometimes referred to as Indigos, Crystals, or Rainbows, are not only more sensitive to chemicals and stimulants, but are also more dramatically affected by others' energies and emotions. This increased sensitivity can be very taxing on the nervous system. I started to understand how to better utilize the gift of my high sensitivity without being drained of energy. The book, *Indigo Adults: Forerunners of the New Civilization* helped me understand that the goal of the Indigo woman is learning to step into her power.

At the same time, I explored other pieces of myself that I had always been curious about. I had always felt drawn to Native American wisdom and customs. Although I have some Native American lineage from my maternal grandfather, I had no direct connection to this knowledge. My grandfather had passed away long before I was born, and my family had not remained in contact with his side of the family. I had always felt a connection to the Native American wisdom and I began to stumble upon pieces of it that grabbed my attention.

On one of my many trips to the bookstore, I found a book that inexplicably drew my attention as I walked by. It was titled *Medicine Cards: The Discovery of Power Through the Way of Animals,* and came with a card deck representing totem animals. Native American wisdom uses the habits of animals to express the truth about our inner selves.

Using the book to understand the totem animal system, I found that my East totem animal is the whale. According to the ancient wisdom, the East totem animal leads you on the path of illumination. The whale is a record keeper; it represents the recorded energy of ancient wisdom and is associated with a tribal legend of an ancient land called *Lemuria*.

Recorded in petroglyphs throughout North America thousands of years ago, the legend tells how the whale once lived on land among the people of *Lemuria*, who were said to be a highly advanced spiritual civilization with gifts of clairvoyance and other supernatural abilities. Their abilities came from the advanced development of their heart center. Their way of life was one of peace and harmony, and their actions and beliefs were results of their amazing, loving hearts. But at some point, a great shift happened on Earth, and the whale retreated to the sea, taking with it the sacred knowledge of *Lemuria*. Before long the waters rose and *Lemuria* sank into the ocean.

Reading further, I learned that 'whale energy people' have DNA encoded with certain frequencies that enable them to access memories of ancient *Lemurian* knowledge. Often they access this information while remaining unaware of its origins. Whale energy people are encouraged to use their voice to open their memory and to express their unique message.

I also signed up for courses and workshops in a variety of esoteric disciplines and began learning from numerous teachers.

I took courses in whatever appealed to me at the time. One class would lead me to another and then another. As I sat with a teacher, I would do my best to openly absorb their style, method, and information. Later, sitting with myself, I observed what resonated with me and kept this wisdom as a guide. What did not resonate with me, I let go of with no judgment. With each new system I studied, I wondered if it would become my main system, but instead found that no single discipline commanded my complete attention. However, every class and teacher that I encountered taught me something that was just right for my growth at that time.

I remember a profound experience when I attended a James Van Praagh workshop. He is a famous medium and I attended one of his weekend seminars in Phoenix along with three hundred other people. I was skeptical and prepared to not connect very deeply. I honestly didn't think I shared any of the skills he had as a channel and intuitive, although my astrology charts, numerology, and animal totems kept telling me that I did.

Nevertheless, I went along with it, doing the exercises he taught us to develop our ability to sense and receive messages from Spirit. Then he paired us with a stranger to test how we were doing by seeing what kind of readings we could get from each other. The woman I worked with was older than me and said right away, "I can tell you right now I won't be able to tell you anything."

Well, we gave it a shot anyway. I held her hands and started to feel her energy. I saw a dog and a cat and felt an immense sadness run through my heart. It was fast, but I trusted it. Because this woman was a complete stranger, I had no fear of being right or wrong, so I went ahead and shared my feelings with her. I figured she would just laugh and we could say we had tried. But as I described my vision, she just started crying and said, "I recently lost my cat and my dog." That was a huge, "Aha!" moment for me. I thought, "I just witnessed something in myself that I didn't really believe in before."

I was now aligning with my search for self and messages began to come in unusual forms with no effort on my part. For instance, I remember the time that I took my daughter for a haircut and when we arrived at the shopping center for her appointment, we found the center filled with healers and teachers participating in a spiritual fair. I laughed with knowing delight, and sent my daughter in for her appointment, while I browsed from booth to booth to see what I would connect with that day.

As I looked around, I found a woman who analyzed people's handwriting to discover personal information. She intrigued me. This was something I had not explored yet, so I took the opportunity to witness her method of teaching.

She had me write a short sentence, and then took a moment to tune into my cursive handwriting. The depth of the information and her insight into my true nature amazed me. One of the first statements she made was, "Very few people know who you really are." Her words touched my heart, and a tear rolled from the corner of my eye as I felt the loneliness exposed by this statement of truth. She went on to tell me that sometimes my heart was too tender for my own good. She told me that sometimes I cared about other people too much, and that I needed to consider myself more in the equation. Astonished by the depth of her analysis, I sat back in my chair and just stared at her. She had confirmed what all the other systems had shown me.

Then, turning the paper over, she asked me to think of a question that I would like answered but to not say it out loud. The question that came to my mind was, "Who am I?"

I watched as she moved the piece of paper over a candle flame on the table between us. She was careful to let the flame gently touch, but not burn, all areas of the paper. Then turning the paper over, she asked me what my question had been. I told her, and she pondered shortly before saying that I had received a lot of information. She proceeded to point to different figures created by the flame on the piece of paper and explained what they represented. Again I gasped at how clearly I could see the figures and how deeply they resonated with me. "This is truly beautiful," I thought.

The first figure was a woman sitting and embracing a child on her lap. This figure represented "a nurturer." The next figure showed a person's head and arms holding a long looking glass up to her eye. This figure represented a "seer or one who can see into the future." The next figure made me laugh. It clearly looked like a clown. The woman said the figure told her that I teach through humor, that I enjoy laughing and entertaining others and that I understand the wisdom of play. Another figure was simply that of a flower. "You are also a beautiful flower," she added. I was deeply touched by the encounter with this wonderful woman, and I told her how much it meant to me. I was starting to learn that the more honest, heartfelt gratitude I felt and shared, the more blessings would be given to me.

The more I opened myself to new experiences and systems of thought, the more my heart opened and my life shifted. With this shift, I started to examine everyday elements of life, beyond the knowledge of formal esoteric disciplines. For example, I left behind competitive sports like tennis, and turned to physical exercise that wasn't centered on competition.

Instead of tennis, I started to dance. I began with ballroom dance and explored many styles including the American rhythm styles of cha-cha, mambo, rumba and East Coast swing. In the American smooth categories, I explored waltz, foxtrot, and tango. Dancing put me back on stage, making my whole body a priority.

Dancing was hard at first. I was uncomfortable on stage at ballroom exhibitions and it was humbling to struggle in a new arena. At the same time it was empowering to know I was brave enough to try something that was awkward and intimidating. In the beginning, it seemed I spent most of my time laughing. When someone asked me why I laughed so much, my answer just rolled out: "I have a choice. I can either laugh or I can cry, as I am humbled by the challenge of learning all of these dance moves. I choose to laugh." Looking back I am grateful that I had the wisdom to develop laughter as a tool I could use when pushing myself into unchartered territories.

My life changed course in 2006 when doctors found black masses in my thyroid. It was a terrifying diagnosis and a real wake up call. After a sonogram and needle biopsy, there was no guarantee that it was not cancerous tissue. It was highly recommended that I have a partial thyroid removal in order to test the masses. My intuition told me that it was not cancer, and the results of the surgery and testing proved my intuition right. I was grateful and relieved to have avoided cancer, but I clearly still had an important lesson to learn. The universe was trying to tell me something.

I had always been more of a holistic person, so I turned to natural methods to heal myself, and to understand the message my body was giving me. Studying medical intuitive systems,

I learned that physical issues begin emotionally. If you do not address the emotions that arise in your life—your wants, needs, and desires—then the emotional form will progress to physical symptoms to let you know that something is not right.

As I read and worked with holistic healers, I received the information from Spirit that it was my fear of speaking up that had catalyzed the growths in my thyroid, those vital glands located in the throat. Truth once again rang clearly as I read the book, *Heal Your Body*, which referenced the relationship between your emotional state and physical symptoms. I was avoiding my true being by suppressing some of my most important gifts. I had not been expressing my truth and my body was trying to let me know that. It was the most pivotal time of my life. It was time to either sink or swim. I realized that if I did not start to live my truths, other more serious physical ailments might arise in an attempt to push me back into alignment with my purpose and truth.

Following the message from my body, I began to speak up more about my own needs. I started by explaining to my husband how I felt and how I was changing. I told him I wasn't happy with our marriage because it was too limiting to me and that I did not feel valued within it. He did not understand when I explained to him that I was becoming involved in the world of Spirit and the healing of others and myself. Already I was speaking a different language and it was very difficult to keep a connection with him. I tried very hard to share my joy in the journey I was going through, but it was slowly dawning on me that we were growing too far apart to be able to stay together.

In her book, *The Age of Miracles: Embracing the New Midlife,* Marianne Williamson emphasizes that a woman cannot remain strong and true to her free and creative self with a partner who stifles or represses her. Williamson's words spoke to me deeply. I remember trying to be myself with my husband, but receiving negative comments, and allowing them to shut me down. I did not understand why, but for a while I allowed myself to be silenced. My lesson was to learn to speak my truth, to stand up for myself, and to not be silenced by others. My lesson was to not give my power away.

Carl Gustav Jung once said, "The most terrifying thing is to accept oneself completely." This was exactly the terror I was experiencing. When we start to explore our true selves, everything around us is called into question. The basis for our relationships has to be reviewed so that we can let go of what no longer aligns with us. I was troubled to find that my husband did not value the authentic me. Having done an enormous amount of soul searching over several years, I realized how important it was for me to have a partner who understands who I truly am and who loves me unconditionally.

It takes courage to not only face your shadows and examine the pieces of yourself that you are not honoring and that are not being honored by your partner, but also to accept how this new understanding is going to change your life. And it was becoming clear how my life was going to change. Perhaps most terrifying of all was the anticipation of how the people closest to me would struggle with these changes.

However, the more I grew in my self-knowledge the more I trusted myself, and consequently, fear lost its power over me. I was starting to fully understand that we are spiritual beings exploring ourselves in a way that can only be done by incarnating physically on earth. We do this in order to experience pain, pleasure, and growth through the choices we make along the way. It is our opportunity to learn who we are. If I tried to protect others by avoiding my own true self, I only hampered their journey through this physical life. We all had important life lessons to learn, and I could not protect anybody from what we all needed to experience.

Shine Your Light

Four

Brave Enough

"Love is the only tool that you need"
—Unknown

One morning in early 2008, I woke up and calmly said to my husband, "Today's the day."

"What?" He was still groggy from sleep, but I could tell he was slowly comprehended what I meant.

"Today's the day we start our own journeys." The words just came out of me. I was calm and sincere but a bit numb as I looked at him. It was something that I just knew was supposed to happen at that moment and I followed my intuition without letting fear or logic get in my way.

The conversation didn't stop there. We got out of bed and began our morning routine. We had been going around in circles for months, and our conversation this morning wasn't much different. We just seemed to talk past each other, each rehashing the arguments that had been made again and again.

In the last several weeks I had observed that we spent most of our time in separate worlds. More than once in the last year I had said to him "You make your choices every day." And as I watched the choices we each made, it was apparent that our journeys were taking us further and further away from each other. When we were together we struggled to speak the same language. He seemed to be fixated on the material world and I was going deeper into the spiritual world. What we valued most were worlds apart, and when I tried to share my world with him I felt I was met with disrespect and judgment.

It was time. I could no longer ignore who I really was.

As we stood in the middle of the bathroom gazing at each other, I knew that our separation was inevitable. I found it interesting that most of our heated emotional conversations took place in the bathroom. I suppose it is one of the places we are most vulnerable, but also most ourselves. After what seemed like a long period of silence, I firmly declared, "It's just not going to work. We need to separate."

He said, "You know this is as good as it gets."

I stood in silence for a while, his words resonating inside me. I was still half shocked that I had laid my desire on the table. It took me a moment to realize he actually thought life couldn't get any better. He still wasn't hearing me.

I shook my head, "I can't live that way. I cannot accept that either one of us will be happy with this being as good as it gets."

I could see he was starting to get irritated. He didn't understand the gravity of the situation, that we had finally hit the fork in our paths. I tried to explain that we could still be friends. He didn't hear me; he just reacted negatively and impulsively.

"This is a failure. It's all your fault. You're ruining everything and screwing everybody up for the rest of their lives." Now he was bringing the children into the conversation. The guilt trip had reared its ugly head. What a test this would be for me. But I would not allow myself to be affected by such statements. I had sat with myself for long enough to know that I was being truthful in my decision. I was not going to let someone else's words trigger guilty feelings in me. I had the power to avoid a guilt trip even when it touched upon the most sacred treasures of my heart; my children.

I responded, "You can believe what you want to believe, but I do not accept that as my truth. If you choose to hang on to that, the only person it is hurting is you. It's not hurting me. I don't think this is a failure. I think we did many beautiful things together. I know that I have not acted my best in recent years in response to our changing relationship. We were only doing the best we knew at the time. But I forgive myself, and I forgive you for the ways you behaved when you were fearful or confused. But it is time to start our separate journeys and I wish you well."

I had tried to take my husband along with me on my journey, but he wanted to stay on his own path. I was done trying to fix what I wasn't supposed to be fixing. We both had a journey ahead of us and our marriage wasn't part of it. I had to trust that my intuition was leading me in the right direction.

It seemed silly that you would stay in a relationship that simply was not working, no matter how hard you tried. And I truly felt that I had tried everything. More than once, counselors and friends had told me when I was still trying to fix things, that I was beating a dead horse.

I was thankful for everything the marriage had brought me, and all the lessons I had learned from it. I gave thanks for all the beauty that it brought, as well as the growth. Part of that growth was an understanding that sometimes your journey is done with a relationship. I just felt that the lessons had been learned and I must move on. I had personally seen that if you try to hang onto something longer than you should, it starts to become more destructive than constructive. I truly felt that the arguments and depression, not to mention a possibility of more health issues due to emotional strain, would just continue to manifest in bigger ways if we continued.

He kept arguing that morning until he left the house, and it took me all week to clear myself of the negative energy that I had absorbed from that intense session. This wasn't the first time. The emotional strain from the pain, fear, and projection of anger made my body limp for at least two days after a big argument. I was unable to gather the energy to pick myself up off the floor and connect to anyone, or to even think clearly enough to function in the physical world. This experience made me very aware of how emotional stress physically drained me.

Months passed and my husband began to understand that I wasn't going to change my mind about splitting up. He started to move forward, realizing I was in a stronger place and that he could not manipulate my emotions with his words. Instead, he began to withdraw from me and close himself off.

Because of his negative energy, I was determined not to fight him during the separation—I knew nothing good would come of it. So I suggested that we do a collaborative divorce, which is conducted through mediation. Everything is presented transparently with third parties present: lawyers, financial experts, and even psychologists.

The psychologist coaches involved in the mediation spent a lot of time with us. My coach said, "You're two years ahead of the rest of them in this process. You seem happy to have more freedom and you feel you are going in the right direction." She was right. I was making tough choices, but I was excited to start living a more authentic life. She said, "You can't expect the kids to be happy right now, because they are not where you are. You started this process two years ago. Give them their time and space to go through their emotions, and to honor their own process."

I was beginning to turn away from fear, embracing trust instead. My life was suddenly on a new path. I discovered that our boundaries are always self-created. I realized that when we become brave enough to step beyond our boundaries, our whole world would shift. For me, this meant I interacted with life in a totally different way: from the home base of love.

I was willing to give up so much in order to gain so much—all based on love and faith.

As my faith grew, I became more aware of the synchronicity of events in my life. I felt the presence and support of something much larger than myself quietly watching over me, standing by and waiting to take my hand whenever necessary.

One day, I was driving down the street, dwelling on the challenges I faced. Just when I needed a bit of support, a Sarah McLachlan song came on the radio. The words from her heartfelt song, "Fallen," spoke to me: "Heaven bent to take my hand to lead me through the fire." Inspired, I understood that I was not ever going to be alone. Spirit had told me that it was present. If I ever needed support, all I had to do was ask, and it would show up. It is hard to put into words the feelings that come during these crystal clear moments of connection.

There was another time when I wanted to talk to a spiritual teacher, Ann, who I had last spoken with over a year ago. I had lost her phone number, and I knew that she had moved. I became fixated on the old piece of paper that I thought contained her information, and obsessively dug through drawers and files for a couple of days. Realizing that I may have thrown out the file during a recent cleaning, I sent out a message to the universe: "I would really like to talk to Ann."

Later that day, as I was walking into a meeting that I knew was going to be emotionally difficult, my phone rang. It displayed an out-of-town number I did not recognize, but I answered it anyway. It was Ann: "I hope that you don't mind me calling you, but you have been popping into my mind for the last couple of days, and I just had to call." I started to laugh uncontrollably. With an enormous boost of confidence, I explained that I would call her back soon and walked into my meeting full of joy and trust. I was learning the power of co-creating my life. I was not in this alone and I never had been. I had just been avoiding the source that we all are connected to.

As the divorce progressed, my ex-husband and I began to divide the physical things in our household. He had bought a house not far away, and was starting to transition into it. One evening, he asked if it were all right if he took the tools that were in the garage. Many of them were special to him because they had been his father's tools, and others were things that he used more often than I did, so I had no problem with his request. The very next week I needed to hang a picture. I went out to the garage and realized I did not have a hammer of any kind. I sort of laughed at myself and went back into the house to do another chore.

The following week was my birthday and my mom called to see what I would like for a gift. I laughed and said that perhaps a hammer and nails and a few other tools would be nice. She didn't quite follow me until I told her the story, and together we found a way to chuckle even during this difficult transitional period. It seemed that even what I wanted for my birthday would be changing into things I had never before considered.

When I finished the loving conversation with my mom, I

decided to escape from the house for a while and have dinner out. I was by myself, since this was my husband's week with the kids. Before long, I was at a local Chinese restaurant, placing an order to go. As I stood in the restaurant waiting for my food, I opened a fortune cookie I had taken from the counter. I have always loved that part of the Chinese dining experience, and gave the little folded piece of paper all of my attention. As I read the fortune, I felt as if someone had knocked the wind out of me. I had to focus and read the words again. The message was clear: "The only tool you need is love."

As I stood there in the middle of the restaurant, I felt an amazing energy run through me. It touched me so deeply that tears swelled in my eyes and I laughed out loud as I fought to catch my breath. It was true. I already had everything I needed. Spirit was showing me that life is simple and I shouldn't get hung up on the small things. When you have love, all the little problems seem much less important. Once you are connected to love, anything extra is just gravy.

Not long ago, I ran across a journal entry I wrote during this phase of my journey. It seemed to sum up what I felt at the time:

"Today is the day that I begin. How did I get to this place? What has it all meant? Where am I going and how? There comes a point when you begin to connect the dots, when the chosen paths begin to mean something, when the picture starts to reveal itself. It is probably not at all what you had envisioned, but somewhere deep inside, perhaps you always knew. The journey was there for a reason. It was there for you and for the others that have traveled along with you. The strength and comfort that comes from that awareness is amazing and beyond words. Once experienced, it becomes the biggest part of you. So let it unfold. Let your life reveal its lessons. Follow your heart, as it will not lead you astray. Find your passion and let its energy run through you in ways you have never experienced. With that, your real life will begin."

Shine Your Light

Five

Even if No One Understands

"I LOVED YOU ENOUGH TO SAY NO EVEN WHEN YOU HATED ME FOR IT. THAT WAS THE HARDEST PART OF ALL."

—ERMA BOMBECK

The kids were shocked. They did not understand. Their world was collapsing before their eyes. Trying to have a calm discussion with the kids was impossible. Sometimes there was yelling, pain, and fear; and other times there was just tears and sadness.

It was time to release the emotions that often accompany what seems like an untimely end to something important in our lives. We felt the sorrow that comes with the passing of an accustomed way of living. I observed that every family member had different emotions to release, their own way of expressing them, and a time line for doing so. Sometimes someone would have a release and it would catch me off guard, because I was preoccupied with my own process and needed the time and space to deal with my own emotions.

I am sure there were things that I could have handled and said better, or even not said at all. But I understand now that we all did the best that we could during a time of tremendous pain and uncertainty. We had never been through such a process and we were all trying our best to find our new footing. No matter how many times you see someone else go through an experience, you cannot understand the gravity until you undergo the same experience.

I'm sure that today we would all see it differently from the way we interpreted it in the moment. I understand now that we were learning important lessons. Today, we all would tell a different story, interwoven with the life lessons we were experiencing. Mostly I remember the flood of emotions that poured out from the depths of each of us, as if we were ripped apart from the inside out.

Occasionally my attempt to console everyone was successful. At first I tried to convince everyone that life was going to be better, because that's how I really felt. But then I realized that I had to let everyone be where he or she was in the experience. We had to generate the bravery individually, bit by bit, to embrace our fate.

There was confusion and many power struggles as we navigated the rapid changes that engulfed our lives. Sometimes the choices made by the kids were not in their best interest, and certain rules had to be enforced. There were moments of anger that made no sense at all. If I tried to logically understand them, it would drive me crazy. I finally realized that a fit of anger or rule breaking was a manifestation of repressed emotions. Sitting down with the kids to address some of their misconducts gave us the helpful opportunity to discuss the real issues behind their behavior.

At one point Samantha, our middle child, began to battle me about her curfew by repeatedly staying out after midnight. "If you can do what you want, then I should be able to do what I want," she spouted. After several discussions and a call from the police telling me she was out after curfew, we were able to get to the root of the issue. Sometimes situations have to escalate to a point that we shout from the bottom of our souls about what is really hurting us. She was finally able to express her pain about the divorce. "Did I still love her?" was the question that came out in different ways. "Was I leaving her?" was another question she asked through tears.

I realized then how important it is to frequently tell your children, in as many ways as possible, how much you love them, especially when going through major shifts. I also realized how important it is to clearly tell your children that a divorce does not mean you are divorcing them. Constantly remind them that your relationship with them is not changing and that you are still there for them. "I will always love you no matter what and I will always be there for you," I assured Samantha. "Nothing could ever change my love for you, little one."

As I wrote this book, I couldn't help but wonder how often we say things that have no relevance to the matter at hand and are really just attempts to express emotions that we have painfully repressed. I wondered how often we build a wall around our hearts in an effort to protect us from pain. The walls do us no good, only serving to block us from our true selves. They merely trap us in with the very issues that need to break free and be released. With any luck we can become aware enough to face these issues and resolve them, instead of allowing them to direct our behavior on a subconscious level.

At one point during the separation, when we were both still living in the same house, I made plans to stay with a girlfriend for the weekend. I told Sophia, our oldest child, "I may need to get out of the house for the weekend. While I am with my friend, I want you to be here with your dad. Things will be more natural if I'm not here. His anger is making it very difficult for me to be here. I just want you to understand that I am not leaving you."

She stared at me with confusion and anger. She hadn't heard this side of things yet, that there was animosity between her mother and father. I had always been very close to each of my children, and yet their father and I had hidden our fights from them. In that moment I realized it had been a poor choice to hide the gradual deterioration of our relationship. Now, the whole thing had come crashing into their lives at once, whereas my husband and I had been stewing on it for what seemed like ages.

"Mom," she said in a blasting voice, "I will never let somebody make me do something that I do not want to do."

I was taken aback, but I was grateful that she was my daughter—that was exactly what I needed to hear. "Wow. Good point," I thought. Her statement really made me look at the way that I was responding to the anger that my husband directed at me. Why was I letting someone bully me? It never ceases to amaze me the things we can learn from our children if we are willing to listen.

Then she continued, "This is my house and no one can make me leave it. I want to be here and I want you to be here with me." Unfortunately, while I did stay in that house after the separation, it was inevitable that my ex-husband and I no longer live together.

Within a few months of separation, my husband moved into another house. I, on the other hand, would remain in the main house, where we had all spent the last seven years. Less than a mile apart, it was easy for the kids to go back and forth between the homes for a week at a time, along with their dog.

To make this transition easier, my ex-husband decorated his new home with the furnishings from our vacation home in Colorado. It was my suggestion: "Perhaps this would make the adjustment somewhat easier for the children." We had spent a lot of time in Colorado over the past few years, and so at least in a small way, trading back and forth between mom and dad wouldn't be completely foreign. Maybe the trappings of familiar physical objects would ease the blow a bit.

On Sunday evenings we would load the car with their backpacks, sports uniforms, the golden retriever, and away they would go. As I waved goodbye, I would think to myself, "Will this ever get easier?" Sometimes I couldn't imagine that it would, but for the most part I knew the pain would find its way out of our lives sooner rather than later. For now, it was just one day at a time.

Things started to get real for our children with the new living arrangements and their biggest emotions emerged. Discussions with my children remained difficult, in spite of my wishes to make the transition as easy as possible. I was now a single parent and found that I had to establish my own rules and enforce them by myself at a time when teenagers are often rebellious. It didn't help that the kids blamed me for the changes and I was not at all prepared for their anger.

Each child reacted differently. Michael, our youngest, was only eleven years old at the time of the divorce. It seemed to me that he spent most of his time just observing everyone else. A sensitive soul, he was sad that the family life was shifting, but he did not express any anger. Somehow, we seemed to know that he was going to be okay, and he knew he was loved very deeply by all of us.

On the other hand, our two daughters had a lot to say. Sophia, who was seventeen at the time, was very vocal about her feelings. After the initial shock, she quickly entered the anger phase and had no problem letting it out. Mostly, it felt like she wanted to vent at me from the top of her lungs. It was good that she felt comfortable being so honest with me, but I was not prepared for her sudden fury.

"I have a right to be angry!" she shouted at me one evening as we talked in her room.

"Yes, you do." I responded. "But you need to do so in a way that is not harmful to yourself or to me."

I was relieved that she could openly express her emotions, and explained to her that it was healthy for her to do so. But when expressing her anger, I told her, it is not healthy to project it at someone else. This situation gave us an opportunity to consciously experience strong emotions and to choose to express them in a healthy way. Of course, it's easier to say that now. Today I also know that whatever lessons we don't handle well will come around again, giving us another chance to make a different choice. The universe constantly gives us opportunities for growth. Sometimes we have to experience the lesson over and over again, wearing ourselves out before we start to work with the lesson and see the gift we are being given.

I am reminded of a statement that I often share: "Learn your lessons fast so they will quit coming back to you."

As she learned to control her unproductive anger, Sophia tried funneling her emotions differently. One evening I spoke with her while she was still struggling with the idea that her life would become different from what she was accustomed. Desperately, she lashed out, "Mom, you made a commitment to be married and you made a commitment to be a mom, and you need to stick to that."

My heart truly went out to her at that moment. I felt her frustration, pain, and confusion. She sat at her desk and I sat next to her on her bed. I looked at what she was working on and thought about the other things in her life she was struggling with.

The college applications she had been meticulously working on for months were spread across her desk. In addition to figuring out which colleges to apply to, she now had to deal with the new family developments. Being an excellent and diligent student, she had created a wide range of possibilities to explore both during and after college.

Surprised at her outburst, I took a moment to gather my thoughts until an authentic answer came to me.

With compassion, I explained, "Yes, I did make a commitment to be married, and yes, I did make a commitment to be a mother. We lovingly chose to have you, and your siblings, and I will always be your mother regardless of what transpires in our lives. And yes, I chose to be a wife. I made the choice that was right for me at the time knowing what I knew then and who I was then. But I have to make the choice that is right for me now, knowing what I know now and who I am now.

"Look at it this way. What if I said to you that you need to pick a major in college, as well as a career, and then you have to stick with it for the rest of your life? You have been so frustrated lately trying to make a decision about what you want to do for the rest of your life. You still have so much to learn about yourself. Right now you can only base your college decisions on what you currently feel is right. Once you go to college, you will change and grow in ways you never imagined. Your earlier ideas may become boring and even unhealthy and as you outgrow them, you'll consider new possibilities. Stop trying to figure out the perfect career for the rest of your life and instead feel what resonates with your inner truth now. We cannot protect ourselves from change and should not fear it. Change and growth are a part of life and sometimes they bring us to places that we never imagined going. The main thing is to tune into your truth in the moment and then you can trust that you will always be on your right path."

The conversation seemed to help her. At least she remained calm and seriously considered what I had said. And as I spoke to her, I spoke to myself as well. Perhaps I was the one that needed to hear those words of wisdom. Today, I am frequently aware that the words we say to one another are often precisely the words that we need to hear ourselves.

As we sat for a moment in silence, I thought about how this wasn't going to be easy but I knew that we would somehow make it through. The pain would be expressed as the struggle continued. The lessons would be explored and growth would come out of it. A certain phrase kept coming to my mind: "They are called 'growing pains' for a reason."

I went on to explain that I completely enjoyed the life I lived as a mother, and was grateful that I was able to have the opportunity to raise three wonderful children. I clarified that I had honored the part of me that was the mother, but had neglected other parts. If I didn't honor all my parts, then I was not showing my children how to be strong, healthy adults. I had honored myself neither as a career woman, nor as an independent individual. I could be all those pieces and still be a responsible mom. In fact, it would make me a better mom.

I explained to all of my children that I was acting as a teacher. My example should be an inspiration, demonstrating how to be brave enough to go out into the world and pursue your dreams. I was showing them how to step beyond fear and convention and to follow your passion even when all the details aren't in focus and no one else understands what you are doing.

Samantha was fifteen years old at the time and had her own unique reactions. When we talked about the divorce, she said, "Mom, everyone I know from a split family is struggling."

I responded, "Well then maybe that is why we are going

through this experience: to show that splitting up a family does not have to be a negative experience. There is still so much we do not understand about what is happening, but maybe we can be an example of making the wise choice to leave a marriage that has failed to provide a loving family environment, and move into a new space that allows us to align with our true selves."

I fully believed this statement with all my heart, which was amazing considering the amount of anger, pain, and confusion that surrounded us at that moment. But I did. For a while it certainly did not look like we were moving into a healthier space, but I had the vision that someday it would all be better for everyone. Blind faith was my anchor and my cheerleader at a time when I desperately needed that kind of support.

Samantha seemed to bottle up the pain and anger inside of herself. I was concerned that this behavior would lead to depression, since I knew firsthand that this is what happens when anger and pain are suppressed.

Thankfully, the kids were able to talk to a psychologist as a part of our collaborative divorce process. The children were lucky to receive coaching on how to express their feelings at a time when the world seemed to be sliding out of control.

Each child had a private session with a psychologist who

prepared a report that was presented to my husband and me during the divorce process. This allowed them to honestly speak their voice to someone other than their parents. A caring and compassionate woman took the time to hear their thoughts and feelings, letting them know that they could talk to her again if they ever felt the need. The sessions were, of course, private, so while I don't know precisely what they discussed, I do know the experience gave them a healthy tool they could use for the rest of their lives.

One of the biggest challenges for the children was growing used to the fact that I would not always be there to answer their questions and to foresee their needs. When it was Dad's week, they had to go to him to discuss what they needed and how they felt, or else rely on each other. I was already starting to see, however, how the challenges were helping us all grow.

Their relationships evolved in ways that may never have happened if things had continued as they were. The family was starting to figure out how to be more independent and resourceful, and how to rely on each other. The kids now helped each other out with car rides, homework, and chores. They seemed to be opening up emotionally with one another and with their father. Even though I noticed this unexpected gift the divorce bestowed upon my children, I could not share my observations. They were in the middle of the growing pains, and weren't in the mood to hear about the so-called "gift of the struggle." Everybody loses sight of the gift of growth when they are in the midst of challenging times.

One day I mentioned to my ex-husband that he should enjoy all of his extra time with the kids. I reminded him what a great opportunity it was: "The girls will be grown and out on their own before you know it. Perhaps you can use this time to create a better bond with them." My words were just met with a grunt. No, he did not yet recognize the gifts of our struggle either.

I also struggled with the big shift of not being with my whole family every day. While they were learning to rely on each other in new ways, I was confronted with the simple basics of single life after seventeen years of being a full time mom. Things like finding health insurance, creating a financial plan, maintaining the house, and just convincing utility companies that I was an authorized account holder who could pay the bills, took up huge amounts of my day.

It took almost a full year to completely separate ourselves from all the things that had tied us together as a family. But the more I focused on disassembling our old life, the sooner I could begin creating a future for myself, and help my children to create their own.

As our family went through these trials and tribulations, the responses coming from extended family and friends were all over the board. I was surprised by the variety of reactions as the news that our marriage of twenty-one years was over.

Some friends were very supportive, knowing how I had tormented myself trying to salvage my deteriorating marriage for the last two years. They knew that my husband and I were spending more and more time away from each other, even in our hobbies. They knew we often took separate vacations. They could see we were making a healthy choice.

The sincerity and directness of some acquaintances surprised me, too. They frankly admitted that the changes occurring in my life were helping them to take a new look at their own relationships. My newfound happiness opened up possibilities in their lives. A few said that they would follow my lead, going their own way once the kids were out of the house. I often found myself wondering how people could stay in an unhealthy or even abusive relationship, solely for the sake of the kids. Others said they wished they had the courage to follow my lead, but knew they could never make it on their own.

I found that by simply being myself I sometimes made others uncomfortable, and consequently some friends just faded away. Perhaps there was judgment, or perhaps there was fear of what they weren't ready to see in themselves. I was definitely getting a crash course in "Not Taking Things Personally." I was realizing that sometimes the other person's feelings are being triggered. Perhaps my decisions were triggering others to start evaluating their lives in ways they were not prepared for.

Recently I was talking with a friend whom I have known for more than ten years. We were talking about writing this book and some of the emotions and experiences that would be expressed in it. When we came to the subject of reactions from others about my divorce, she very directly told me how she had judged me when she had first learned of my divorce. She had been aware of how unhappy I was and what a struggle my marriage had been for quite a while. Even so, she had still judged me harshly for initiating the divorce.

I've had to learn to not care too much about what people think of me. To do so is to give my power away. If you are concerned with getting others to believe what you believe, or to feel a certain way, then you are letting them control your behavior. If you are looking for validation outside of yourself, you are giving your power away.

Eventually the responses and reactions to my divorce began to sap my energy. I found I could no longer take the time and expend the energy to try to explain myself to everyone. It wasn't my job to help them understand. Rather than defend myself, I needed to conserve my energy to focus on moving forward with my life. Slowly but surely, I learned that the only validation that mattered came from myself.

Shine Your Light

Six

Naked

WHO AM I?

As my divorce completed, and I transitioned out of my old life, I found myself in a strange place. It is a hard state of being to describe. It felt like when you wake up in a strange room while traveling—a momentary disorientation, those few seconds in the hotel bed when you just can't place where you are. I often felt as if I were standing naked in the middle of a crowded room, my mind empty, with everyone waiting to see what costume I would put on.

I had shed a deep layer of identity composed of many different roles that had determined the nature of my existence. Now this old stuff had come off, as if I had shed my very skin, and it lay beside me like a pile of clothes. The sudden depth of my vulnerability stunned me. I had no roles to hide behind any longer. I was no longer a wife, or a partner. I was no longer part of a community of married couples, or of a happily married family with children. Although I was in the same place physically, it felt as if I had just entered the scene as a whole new character, but without a script of the story line going forward.

In place of my lost identities, I had only questions. Was I going to go back to work? If so, what kind of work would I do? Did I want to date? Even the basics were up for debate, like was I going to move, or stay in the old family house? Not to mention, of course, the big question that remained in front of me but which now screamed even louder: Who Am I?

But my mind was empty, blank, and clueless. I had been unaware of my own needs and desires for so long, that in my nakedness not even the simplest information came easily. I remember filling out some sort of questionnaire that asked what my favorite music and movies were. I was stumped. "Hmm…" I thought to myself, "What is my favorite color or song or movie?" I could tell you what my son's favorite movie was, or what music my daughters listened to, but I couldn't tell you mine. The sensation was disarming, but also interesting.

I was again met with the reality that I had valued everyone else's opinions more than my own. I had created an imbalance in my life by being more of a giver than a receiver. I began to understand that if I did not value myself I would ultimately have less to give, and this was not useful to anyone in the long run.

During this time I had the same vision again and again whenever I shut my eyes. There was a fairy-like young girl hopping over a body of water. Each time she jumped into the air, she hung there for a moment until a lily pad magically appeared in the water before her, allowing her to land. She was calm and playful, with no fear that a safe landing would be provided. But more than that, she seemed to be creating the path of lily pads by herself, one hop at a time. Her path was a process of calm observation and rhythm, and an ability to remain present in the moment as she sensed her intuitive desires and confidently created the next lily pad.

This clear vision somehow gave me the confidence to mimic her behavior. I began to trust my leaps of faith, confident that the next step would be presented to me as I needed it. I was creating the path of my journey and I simply had to make a choice of which direction I wanted to go in order to see where to place my foot.

At this time, it often felt as if my biggest obstacles were the voices of those around me. They were just as disarmed as I was by my sudden lack of identity. Friends, acquaintances, and relatives—they all had something to say about my newfound freedom.

A conversation that often came up was the topic of work and

employment. After years of supporting a working husband, their concern was understandable. People would ask what I planned to do for work, and what I had done in the past. I explained that I had a degree in accounting and had worked as an auditor before I became a full time mother seventeen years ago. At that point we would usually laugh together as they said, "You don't seem like an accountant to me." They were right—that role didn't fit me anymore.

And yet the conversation almost inevitably turned to, "Well, you had better take some accounting refresher courses so that you can get back into the work force." I was puzzled that people would suggest I go back into a field they had just acknowledged did not suit me. I suppose they thought of it as the safe way to make a living, but to me it just sounded like a fear-based decision. I had learned that making a decision based in fear was the lowest level of decision-making. A silence usually followed in these conversations when I explained that I was actually not going to pursue accounting, but in fact, I planned to follow my passion for natural healing and spirituality. Their silence confirmed their unstated fears, but I would not let it affect my decision.

I had become a people person, and though I still had an analytical side, the idea of sitting at a desk sounded like torture to my soul. I remember an inspiring quote from years ago: "When you work with people you have to learn to be effective, not efficient." That is what motherhood had taught me: how to step beyond the "bottom line" and instead approach a problem or goal with compassion and understanding. The last seventeen years had taught me the importance of combining my analytical, male energy, with my feeling, female energy.

I was at a unique point in my life where I could see the value of all the roles I had played so far, and understood how each one had developed just the right skill to add to the basket that formed a more complete me. I had the confidence and the skills to work towards a precise vision of myself in the long term as a healer and teacher.

This wasn't something that could happen overnight, though. I was fortunate that through the divorce agreement, I was to receive financial support during my transition into a new career. But it wouldn't last forever. I had some assets from the division of our marital property, but I now had to plan for my long-term future, as well as make equal contributions to our children's upbringing.

Sometimes people stay in relationships out of fear that they cannot support themselves. It takes strength to believe that you can be on your own. Even if you have some assets, it takes courage to know that you can manage what you have to provide for yourself. I had found that strength by first stepping away from an unhealthy relationship. Continuing to trust my wisdom, I knew I could take care of myself as I aligned with my truth, power, and connection to the universe.

So I knew what I would do for a living, even if it would take some time and faith to achieve. On the other hand, when it came to dating, I was in unexplored territory.

When my wedding ring came off, I began getting a lot of attention. It was a big surprise. I had been a faithful wife, and so was very unfamiliar with the energy of being single. The shift happened dramatically, as I suddenly began projecting and receiving the energy of being "available." I observed the change and did not let it overwhelm or frighten me. Instead, the new energy was something I found interesting to observe. Spirit put the energy in my path, and so I felt the need to explore it.

I started to experiment with dating again, but the dating scene was completely foreign to me. I had been in a relationship with the same man for twenty-seven years—twenty-one as husband and wife! It felt like everything had changed since my last date, and I was completely out of the loop. There were so many rules and expectations that completely surprised me: when to text, when not to text, what to talk about, and what to avoid in conversation. The list went on and on. It felt like I needed a refresher course: "Dating in the New Millennium, for Dummies."

When I talked with friends about dating, I received so many suggestions. I would just laugh and say, "I'm not going to do that!" I kept thinking, "Who made up these rules and why are we following them?" For instance, I kept running across the recommendation that women should go and do things that guys like to do in order to be around them. Whether you liked motor-cross racing or not, you should go to a race, because this is where you could find a large number of men. How ridiculous! I had stripped my old identities until I was now "naked," and I was certainly not about to put on any roles that were inauthentic.

I had a much simpler approach that would allow me to enjoy being myself—it was the basic "like attracts like" theory. There would be no false advertising. I would do the things I enjoyed, focusing on keeping myself happy and remaining true to myself. I figured the right person would be the person attracted to the real me. If I worked on myself, the rest would fall into place.

Often, when people step out of one relationship, they feel like they need to immediately step into another. When you understand that like attracts like, you will discover that moving too quickly from an old relationship that involved pain and tribulation will only lead you back into a similar situation. I knew I didn't want to attract the energy I was still processing from my divorce, so I put myself on the sideline to avoid attracting somebody who was also going through a similarly vulnerable change.

I remained single and devoted to myself for almost two years, undoing my old life, and deeply processing what I had learned so that I did not have to repeat those lessons on my new path. Whenever I did meet someone, as I occasionally would, they tended to be people who were in the middle of their own transitions and still needed to do the work of healing and growing before entering another relationship. I saw this demonstrated by hard facts while attending the Arizona State course on divorce: the period of time between divorces and remarriage was surprisingly short, and consequently the rate of divorce for a second marriages was much higher than a first marriage.

Sitting quietly alone is often a hard thing to do, and that is why people have a tendency to avoid it at all costs. But if you can be still, Spirit starts to show you all your "stuff." This can be difficult, but the truth is that you cannot run from it. Spirit will bring up important issues again and again until you choose to examine them.

Fortunately, I had a quiet and familiar place to sit with my lessons. My career and dating life may have been unchartered territory, but at least I had the sanctuary of my familiar home to be present with my new self. This was the house where our little ones had grown into teenagers, and where we had shared celebrations too numerous to count. We had spent years renovating this house to make it our home, with a beautifully landscaped backyard, a swimming pool and basketball court, and even a sunken trampoline. Though I was ready to walk away from it, I stayed for the time being at my children's request. It served as an excellent home base for all of us until the next step came into sight.

My favorite thing about this house was its proximity to Mother Nature. It was a good-sized ranch house and our land, well over an acre, bordered the Pima Indian Reservation. It was away from the city lights and at night was lit only by the bright stars in the sky. Being on the edge of developed land in the desert was a bit like living in the "animal kingdom," because of all the wildlife that paraded through our yard and sometimes even through our house.

The howls of coyotes and the neighborhood bobcat had been around for years. It wasn't uncommon to see a herd of wild pigs stroll along the street at dusk. At night, the local owl sometimes hooted down our chimney, sharing crickets and grasshoppers that happened to slip from its claws. Around the house, it was not uncommon to be surprised by scorpions, tarantulas, and even rattlesnakes!

During married life, these occasional encounters woke us up from our everyday routines, adding some spice and excitement. Now and then, when a family member felt the need to kill a small soul—a spider, for instance—I actually felt its pain. I often asked myself, "Why is it that we find the need to kill out of fear?" I am grateful for having those experiences. They helped me to consider the feelings of all living things and now I am more conscious about how I treat them.

It was after the divorce, though, that I really began to be called by the nature that surrounded me. Once, my ex-husband even had to help me try to evict a baby rattlesnake that had invaded the kitchen cabinets. We tore the place apart looking for it, and later the repairman looked at us like we were crazy. Perhaps these animals were trying to tell me something. Perhaps I wasn't supposed to be pushing them out, but instead following them to new environments.

One afternoon during this phase, I sat in my lounge chair in my beautiful backyard full of nature, surrounded by silence, except for the chorus of birds singing their unique songs. The wide-open sky seemed limitless and gave me plenty of room to breathe. The wind was refreshingly cool and gently nurtured my soul. It was springtime and the desert was in full bloom.

I meditated on that beautiful spring landscape of the Sonoran Desert. It had always amazed me how the desert could sometimes be so desolate and barren, and at other times, so amazingly green, full of color and life. The cacti, revealing their delicate flowers nested between rows of thorns, caught my attention, and I thought of the desert as a place where brutal heat burns away what is no longer useful. From the ashes emerges a whole new being. It represented the phoenix rising, which, in a way, seemed to be what was happening to me.

As I sat there, I returned to that all-important question. I directed it to Spirit: "Who Am I?" This is what came to me:

"And so it is for me

...the bird...

...to be free as a bird...

...to be happy as a lark...

...to be light and free of baggage...

...to be willing to go where the wind blows me...

...to nurture and cuddle with my little ones...

...to soar, to glide, to twirl and to enjoy the gift of feeling the wind beneath my wings...

...to sing a beautiful tune that only I can sing, knowing that others will hear my song and enjoy it, and that those

with whom it resonates will respond to me, grateful for the
deep connection that is truly one of the
greatest experiences of life."

This was a wonderful moment of reconnecting to who I
was at the deepest soul level. Not only was Spirit showing me
my inner self, Spirit was showing me my future. I have always
connected to the bird as the "messenger of Spirit," as well as to
the wind that carries the bird's song, connecting Spirit to Earth.

I don't know if it was the setting of my familiar, natural
backyard, but I had asked and Spirit was giving me the same
message: I am here to be a messenger, to teach others by example,
to grow and to learn and to spread my wings; to be happy and
let go of all that had served its purpose; to follow where Spirit
leads and to nurture those looking for the compassion and
encouragement to spread their own wings.

It was this act of openly questioning without expectations that
continued to point me to who I truly was and to the lessons that
I was here to learn. If I needed answers, I would focus intently
on a question to Spirit, learning how to talk to Spirit as if I were
talking to myself. Then I would listen with an open mind, with
no preconceived ideas, and being careful not to judge myself
when the answer came back. Sometimes the messages would

come to me directly and sometimes they would come through other teachers or healers. Regardless of how I received the message, I found I was the one who had to initiate the contact, and then Spirit simply appeared.

I have since realized that not everyone will connect with Spirit and find answers in the same way that I do. Some people access this process by going to the golf course or hiking in nature. Sometimes the conversation with Spirit is more formal, through the guidance of a religion, therapists, or teachers. At other times, informal and unexpected connections will give you answers. I believe that there is no right or wrong way to connect with this interconnected power and it is part of your journey to find your own language. I was slowly beginning to find mine.

Shine Your Light

Seven

Spirit Calls

"MY LESSON WAS TO LEARN TO BE FLEXIBLE LIKE
THE PALM TREES. I WOULD LEARN TO BEND
BUT NOT BREAK.
—JOURNAL ENTRY, 2009

My divorce was complete by the end of 2008. The children would spend the first week of the New Year with their father, and I didn't want to be alone around the holidays. As a present to myself, I bought a ticket to Hawaii to spend the New Year's holiday with my aunt and uncle on the North Shore of Oahu.

It was a great opportunity to be nurtured by the energy of the islands. Hawaii's powerful, creative female energy always embraced me and nurtured my soul with its tenderness. After such a long, hard year of emotional strain, my soul was certainly in need of recharging.

As I stepped off the plane, I was met by the lush green landscape and the caress of the warm island wind. After the dry desert climate, the moisture in the air was like a kiss upon my face. The rhythm of the people, and their gentle communication made me feel as if all were safe in the divine order. Worries, struggle, and hurry left me and I felt only abounding peace and grace.

I was grateful for the warm welcome of my aunt at the airport. Just ten years older, she is a joyful soul who lifts me up with her buzzing energy. She immediately began to lay out the fun she had planned for my visit: a girl's night out, beautiful beaches, a cookout with my uncle, and of course, plenty of laid back down time. She also told me about a casual acquaintance, a woman who had expressed interest in talking with me. She was a counselor and my aunt thought that I might enjoy meeting her.

As it turned out, the weather was rather rainy during my stay. But this didn't prevent me from enjoying a vacation of peaceful moments and joyful socializing. It wasn't until the last day of my trip that I met the woman my aunt had mentioned—the woman who would become my next teacher.

On my last evening on-island, a dinner engagement fell through. I mentioned to my aunt that it just wasn't meant to be, and instead suggested that we try to meet up with Susan, the friend she had mentioned who wanted to meet me. A quick phone call and we had plans to meet her for a walk on the beach that evening. I was starting to notice the synchronicity of events: when one door shuts, it was often because there is a better door to walk through.

Susan met us at my aunt's house, and the moment I saw her, a shiver of excitement ran up my spine. Almost instantly I sensed that she was a spiritual teacher; in fact, she was the very teacher I was looking for. As they say, when you are ready for a teacher, the teacher will appear.

In Hawaiian, Susan is called a kahuna, which means a keeper of ancient spiritual knowledge. The word kahuna is also used to denote a chief, or leader, as well as a shaman-like figure. Although she represented herself as a counselor to the general public, I realized what she was immediately. Susan had been trained by her grandmother to carry on the sacred Hawaiian traditions, but she kept her true identity private. She did not have a business card, website, or social media presence. Those who were to find her would be connected by the mystery of the universe directing their way.

As we walked the beach, we fell into a discussion of ancient Mayan wisdom. I had recently been drawn to the topic of the Mayan calendar, which was getting mainstream attention for predicting the end of the world in late 2012. It turned out that Susan frequently taught Mayan wisdom, and so we found ourselves still on that subject long after the sun had set. My aunt had wandered home, leaving us to our deep esoteric conversation.

Like me, Susan didn't believe 2012 was a literal end of time. She explained that the Mayan calendar grid is an explanation of the rise, or evolution, of consciousness. She showed me how 2012 and the surrounding period is a time of tremendous growth for humanity. We both felt that this is not a doomsday event, but a part of our collective evolution.

I enjoyed our conversation and was surprised when Susan called the following morning to ask if I would like to study with her. During her morning meditation, she had received guidance that she was to work with me. I was honored and grateful and began to wonder whether meeting her was the purpose of my Hawaiian holiday. Spirit was leading me forward one step at a time, even when I wasn't looking for it. However, if I remained open and observant, I was conscious enough to understand what the universe was offering me.

After my visit to Oahu in January of 2009, I continued to work with Susan over the phone for a few hours every two weeks. It was a time for me to learn to be a teacher while being the student. We focused on learning deeply about myself. It was a guided inward journey to discover where all the pain and lessons grew, in order to understand my life's path. Hopefully I could then share my knowledge and personal experiences with others who might face similar crossroads and lessons.

One morning I had another moment of knowing while sitting in my kitchen, gazing out on the colorful desert landscape illuminated by a rainbow of spring flowers. I sat in silence, and the knowing simply presented itself, like a feeling in the gut that spoke directly to me.

I was being drawn to Hawaii again, but it felt as if this time I would be staying for longer. The feeling resonated with me, and my inner compass presented the message like an old wise soul offering me the next step on my path. It seemed crazy, but at the same time, it felt so right. It felt like I was being called home.

As I looked out the window I realized instantly that I would be getting on a plane with a large suitcase to fly over an ocean for reasons that I could not fully explain to anyone else. But there I was. I would continue my leaps of faith into the unknown, relying on my soul to lead me to its new meaning. Trusting my intuition was a muscle that I was learning to flex more frequently. I had certainly given it plenty of exercise lately, and now it was ready to take me on an even longer journey.

The changes I was embracing were big enough for me, but they were enormous for my family. It felt like I kept flipping the boat. I would wait until everyone was accounted for, albeit dripping wet, and then tip the boat again. I did not want to push anyone faster than they could handle, but we had to let go in order to flow with the current of the river.

At first I kept the knowing of my journey mainly to myself. On occasion, I would tell a stranger that I was moving to Hawaii to see how it felt without having to go into some big explanation. I find it is sometimes easier to talk to strangers who have no expectations than it is to talk about change with someone we know. More often than not, I was met with surprised smiles and friendly encouragement, which told me I was making the right choice.

In the summer of 2009, I returned to Hawaii with Samantha and Michael, my two youngest children, for two weeks. I wanted to give them the gift of the warm nurturing sun on their faces, the soft sand between their toes, and the ocean waves calling them to play. We went to be cradled in the arms of a simple summer life full of laughter. Sophia would not be joining us, as she was already busy creating a new life after high school, complete with a summer job and her own travels.

One of the reasons I brought Samantha and Michael to

Hawaii was to present them with the possibility of living there with me. Unlike Sophia, who would be leaving to go to college in the fall, they were both going to have to make the decision of where they wanted to live. I made sure they understood that the choice was completely their own, and if they did join me, I would make their needs (such as school) a priority when choosing where to live. I wanted them to know that they were active participants in the journey, and that they had a voice in the matter. I explained that their father and I both loved them very much and would always be there for them no matter what they chose.

Inevitably, emotions flared up as this conversation began. Anger, fear, and pain were reactivated and it felt as if we were back in the midst of the initial separation from a year and a half before.

Michael was clear that he was not interested in moving to Hawaii. I wasn't surprised that my teenage son wanted to stay on the mainland with his friends and father. I knew in my heart that it was the right choice for him. At his age it was important to be spending more time with his father, and Hawaii did not tug at his soul as it did mine.

Samantha, on the other hand, became extremely upset. She and I are very close and similar in many ways. And while she, too, resonated with the island life of Hawaii, she did not want to move away from her friends for the last two years of high school.

The decision seemed to break her heart, and she had many conflicting emotions. She really wanted me to stay with her on her journey, rather than joining me on mine. Our heated conversations rehashed the difficult discussions we had gone through with the divorce.

"I want to stay with my friends and I want you to be there with me," she expressed, clearly from her heart.

I reminded her, "I love you and I will always be there for you. Our journeys may take us in different directions for a while, but I am always there for you."

We were both learning that we couldn't control the path that others choose to take, and that we must allow everyone to follow the call of his or her own journey. But in the moment, we had trouble understanding that our personal growth required our daily lives to be separate. All that we could see was the loss of the everyday moments we enjoyed sharing. It was tough, to say the least, and the pain enveloped us all as we grappled with our new future.

Of course, in hindsight, it is easier to see the benefits that came during our time together in Hawaii. I had asked my teacher Susan to spend some time with each of my two "little ones" to assist them however they needed. I felt so blessed to have a compassionate soul who could listen to, nurture, and guide them. Susan helped them experience how to accept change they couldn't control, and to express their feelings in healthy ways. In particular, she encouraged my daughter to write a letter to me explaining the situation from her point of view.

My daughter jumped on the idea, and delivered a letter expressing her feelings while asking for acknowledgement of her desires. Her letter was a wonderful gift to both of us, demonstrating how to effectively share emotions. When you are in the middle of a difficult transition, honest communication and acknowledgement from loved ones is very important. Writing a letter helped my daughter distance herself from her actions and find clarity in her feelings.

Following the call of Spirit in making a transition to Hawaii was not easy or smooth. My children had emotions to process, and I had to work hard to ensure their voices were heard. I told them I was proud of where they were in their personal journeys, and reminded them that I wouldn't be making such a big change if I didn't know they were ready for it.

My ex-husband was just as difficult to communicate with. We weren't sharing information with each other well, and it came as a shock when he realized he would be with the kids 100% of the time. To his credit, when this finally sunk in, he accepted and embraced it. From there, we all started to move forward in our own way.

And so my journey continued, asking me to do the hardest thing of all: leave my children. My astrology chart had warned that I would sometimes hold the world closer to my heart than my immediate family. I seemed to be the only one who understood what this meant, leaving many people who could not support my choices. Their additional judgment made the transition even harder.

I kept trying to take everyone with me on my journey: first my husband, then my kids, and finally my friends. But a big part of the journey was realizing that I had to learn and grow on my own. I rediscovered a book I had bought years ago—*The Secrets and Mysteries of Hawaii* by Pila Chiles—and things began to make sense.

The book had sat forgotten on my bookshelf for years, but now its pages seemed to contain the answers to all the questions I had. It describes the island of Oahu as the throat chakra of the Hawaiian islands. The concept of chakras comes from the Hindu and Buddhist traditions, in which each chakra corresponds to a different energy-processing center of the body. There are seven main chakras, and each has a different purpose.

The fifth chakra—the throat chakra—is the energy center for communication. *The Secrets and Mysteries of Hawaii* emphasizes how the voice of Hawaii comes from Oahu, where eighty percent of the population resides. This voice, Pila writes, is shifting away from male dominance back to its original female softness. During this time of transition, people should be listening to their own true voices and learning the things about themselves that needed to be articulated. As the island transforms, so would the residents, in a joint process of development.

Pila Chiles is of Cherokee descent and he associated this transformation of the islands with the turquoise blue of freedom cherished by his native culture. In Cherokee traditions, turquoise is gifted to those who blossomed into their true selves, and the new soul would be encouraged to focus on the blue mineral as they would on the sky. The blue sky called them to lift their wings like the eagle and fly from the earthly realm to go discover the reasons for their existence. So too, writes Pila, does Oahu call to those searching for their true voice.

As I read all of this, I was floored. There it was, laid out before me. I was being lead to the island of the female voice and directed to connect to the color of "sky blue," which serendipitously was the color I had been seeing for the last few years when I closed my eyes. I had told very few people of this vision of sky blue, and yet here was the explanation.

As the summer ended and the kids got ready for school, I prepared for my adventure across the ocean. It was surprisingly simple, actually, given the scope of my next step. The biggest hurdle was shipping my car to Hawaii, since I still had a lease on it and didn't want the extra expense of renting a car on Oahu. Meanwhile, I left my house as it was—I wouldn't rent it out since I didn't know how long I would be gone, and it would be a good home base for visiting the children.

I had some funds to live off until I could start making my own income, but it was still a risk. I had a car and house payment to keep current on, as well as the kid's expenses and college tuition. But I maintained my faith that I would be able to bring in my own income doing work that came from my heart. I just had to believe that I was building something I couldn't entirely see yet. I was following my passion and I knew if I was brave enough, I could not go wrong.

Once more I boarded a plane to Hawaii. I had just two suitcases containing clothes, my camera, my computer, and a few books. I tried to bring the cat, but Samantha was adamant, "You are not taking the cat with you." Fair enough. The cat and the dog stayed with the kids and I was off, completely on my own.

If anyone had told me two years before that I was going to be living in Hawaii, I would have said they were crazy. Hawaii is a place you go to visit. It's a bunch of small, isolated islands, and it wasn't where I wanted to be at the time.

But when I did move, it instantly felt like home. I knew it was the only place I was supposed to be at that moment. It was comforting and nurturing. The environment was extremely healing and exactly what I desperately needed after all that I had been through. I had been absorbing everyone's emotional energy, and it was time for me to do my own healing and put myself first.

When I talked with people about my move, I had explained that I could not express what was going on yet, but that I would someday be able to tell my story in a book. I was worn out and tired of explaining myself. In Hawaii, I no longer had to explain myself. I had been giving my power away by allowing myself to be absorbed with what "they" thought. I could now focus on what I wanted to create for myself.

It was still a journey, taking one step at a time as the choices appeared before me. In my heart, I knew I was doing what was right for me and for the higher good of everybody else. All I needed was the faith to lead me to a place that would be greater for all. Nobody feels the same thing at the same time as anybody else. As I embraced the realization that everyone processes their feelings in their own way, Spirit put the last piece of the puzzle in place.

Even though I had initially been called to Hawaii by Spirit to learn from a kahuna and absorb the healing energies, Spirit had more in store for me. Through my intuition and through signals from several other teachers, I was getting another message. I was going to Hawaii to teach.

I didn't understand it in the moment, because I felt so far away from being a teacher and a leader. But as I had learned to do, I sat with the feeling that I would teach and just observed it. I had faith that I would understand it better when the time had come for the universe to lead me to that path. What I needed to do now was be brave enough to follow my instincts no matter what sort of wild goose chase they led me on.

Shine Your Light

Eight

Exploring Me

"You have to be lost to be found."
—Journal Entry, 2009

I had been at my aunt's house in Oahu for no more than a couple weeks before I flew to California to help my oldest daughter move into college. She and her father had loaded up the SUV with all she needed for her new life and driven her to San Diego. After he left, we planned to meet up at the hotel I was staying at in Mission Bay.

As I waited for her near the lobby that fronted the bay, I basked in the warm ocean wind rushing past me. It felt wonderful to breathe the fresh air, and to be outside and present in this moment when our lives were about to cross again. I felt like there were no limitations, and both my daughter and I had broad futures. Before long she was striding briskly out onto the deck where I was waiting.

With an edge of hostility, she shot a question at me: "So is this how it is going to be now? We just meet up at random places around the world?"

I smiled faintly at this new woman standing before me. "Yes," I responded, "and does that seem so terrible?"

After a moment of silence, I continued, "My job now, as your mother, is to teach you to be a woman of the world, to go out into the world and not be afraid to follow your passions, even when they take you on a wild journey. I do not need to be by your side anymore. A mother's job is to teach her children to fly on their own, and I know that you are ready for that freedom."

My words must have touched her heart, because she seemed to immediately relax and absorb my feelings. How could she argue with me when she knew that I was helping her to stand in her own power, and was telling her that I saw her strength and readiness even if she didn't? The moment of reflection passed with no more words, and we shared a long and loving embrace. It was one of those embraces that matter so much during challenging times, reaching out from the bottom of our hearts to comfort each other.

That weekend with my daughter flew by before we knew it. We were consumed with hauling luggage up to her dorm, learning our way around the campus, and meeting new roommates and friends. It was thrilling, scary, happy, and sad—a constant up and down. But any big change is a roller coaster of emotions, isn't it? Growing takes tremendous courage and the ability to stay grounded when others might not.

By Sunday, I knew my daughter was happy and that she had plenty of support in her new life. I also knew that no matter what I had going on in my life that I would be there for her when she needed me. An ocean was never going to be an issue if my children needed me, and I reminded them of this constantly.

I was delighted that we had this opportunity to experience our new "mature" relationship. She was stepping into an independent role and I was cheering her on. "Fly away little one," I said to her in my soul, "I know that you will be fine."

Meanwhile, I too, had to fly away and discover my new life. As I returned to Oahu, once again the words, "You have to be lost to be found," echoed through my mind. Perhaps I was starting to understand the fact that losing myself was actually helping me to find myself.

It was time to find my own place to live. On Craig's list I found a very small, but cute, short-term rental close to the beach that was fully furnished. I laughed as I walked past the underwater mural painted on the outside of the unit, only to find the interior walls also filled with aquatic creatures; it felt as if I was walking into a cartoon. As I envisioned myself sharing the small breakfast table with the brightly colored octopus on the nearby wall, I couldn't help but think that the universe was trying to tell me to lighten up a little.

I signed the contract with the knowledge that I was being led by Spirit to take the next step with this short-term commitment. It was not easy for me to make a decision that meant less long-term stability. It was wonderful to be living so freely in the moment, but in other ways I felt like I did not have enough ground to stand on to see which way to go. I was learning to trust what came to me in every moment, and only embracing what truly spoke to my soul.

But there I was. I moved into my new place in less time than most people take to enjoy a good meal. It doesn't take long to park your car and unpack two suitcases. Although I had enjoyed the company of my aunt and uncle for a couple of weeks, it felt good to be on my own on the other side of the island.

My adventure continued and now I was ready to do some more "work." The freshness and freedom of being in a new place made it easier to open to the possibilities of redefining myself. Since I was still learning to stand on my own, I stayed away from dating and found other ways to get back into the swing of social life.

Since bars and clubs do not attract me, I returned to my love of movement by exploring the dance world of Honolulu as a way to meet others socially. In Scottsdale, I had taken American Ballroom classes and even participated in a few exhibitions. They had been wonderful for several reasons. They put me on stage, taught me to be in the moment, and helped me to feel comfortable in the close embrace of a man once again.

I started with a ballroom class in Honolulu, but it didn't last long. In Hawaii, ballroom dance just felt too structured. My body and spirit wanted more room to freely express themselves and respond to the music from deeper in my soul.

One day after class, as I was taking off my shoes and packing up to go home, a large crowd of fun and energetic people starting filing through the door. The strong beat of salsa music began to pulse through the room, and in moments the dance floor was packed. Moving in unison, the dancers began to practice their warm-up exercises.

"Wait a minute," I thought to myself, "I think I'm going to stay." I went back on the dance floor and joined in the energy, finding that the beat of the music stimulated my mind and body and pushed me out of my box. The beat enticed me to practice the sensual movements that I hadn't dared in a long time.

"Why was that?" I thought to myself. Why did I give up my role as a sensual woman somewhere along the way? I found it invigorating, and so I kept going to the salsa classes as often as possible. The more I continued with salsa, the more I allowed myself to let my hair down and step into the ownership of myself as a mature woman. At the same time, I was meeting wonderful friends who shared my playfulness and adventure that came as a natural part of dancing in high heels to exciting music.

I couldn't stay away from ballroom for long, however. Hawaii has a large group of International Ballroom dancers. Having only studied American Ballroom on the mainland, I thought it would be exciting to experience the other style of ballroom dancing, known as International Ballroom, while I had the opportunity. This dance community was made up of people from a wide array of Asian and Pacific Island cultures. Hawaii is a place where many cultures live side by side, maintaining their independence, while also interacting peacefully and respectfully. I loved meeting all the different people in a merging of the East and West. We even enjoyed a variety of ethnic foods at the ballroom, while people chattered away in exotic languages that I wished I could speak

So there I was: a blond in the middle of a crowd of shorter, mostly dark skinned, dark haired people. My dance partner was an energetic Chinese man whom I towered above, especially when I put on my dance shoes. He was a never-ending source of energy and spunk. He once said to me, "It is never hard to find you even when there are over a hundred people in the room. You are the swan in the middle of all the ducks." His charming sense of humor brought a smile to my face and made it easy for me to embrace my uniqueness, instead of feeling out of place.

From International Ballroom classes I was drawn to the West Coast swing crowd. This style brought in the playful whimsy of creative expression. Although it was still a partner dance, it gave more room for the woman to find her voice and self-expression. As you can imagine, it worked well for me. It was fun, it was playful, and it still took a respectful partnership to express it.

Eventually I was led to Argentine Tango. My heart was captured within minutes of hearing the music and seeing this dance in action, which spoke directly to my soul. As a Taurus, I am all about romance, sensuality, and tender touch. Argentine Tango holds all of these.

Argentine Tango requires you to move with your immediate feeling of the music, and to embrace your free, creative expression. The man frames the movements, initiating them, and then graciously offering the movement to the woman. The woman can accept or reject that movement, after which he responds with the next point in the "conversation." There is no communication beyond tuning into each other's physicality and responding intuitively, based on your feelings in the moment. I felt this to be a positive, free-flowing, female-male energy conversation. There were no right or wrong answers and it wasn't pre-formatted. Such a creative relationship helps you to live in the moment. In fact, it's absolutely necessary in order to successfully connect with your partner.

Others started to notice the transformation I was experiencing while exploring these new styles of dance. During a trip back to Scottsdale to visit my children, I had the opportunity to take a dance lesson, and for the first time saw how others perceived my change.

During a West Coast swing lesson, the man I was dancing with seemed attracted to me in a way that perplexed him. He kept asking me questions, trying to know more about me, giggling all the while as this strange energy drew him to me. Little did he know, I had danced with him before. When I mentioned to him that we had danced some time ago, he threw back his head and laughed out loud, emphatically stating that we had never met. "I would never have forgotten that smile," he added. That was just before he jokingly asked me to marry him. I had danced with him less than a year before, when I had not yet stepped into my fullness and new self. Now my energy was so different that he did not remember me at all.

I realized that when we do our inner work, it changes how the outer world responds to us. I was amazed that someone who did not remember we had met before could be so inspired by my new energy and openness. Though this shift was a bit disarming, I must say it was rather fun receiving compliments and marriage proposals. In a text that he sent to me awhile after that particular night, he admitted that he had a crush on me. I responded, "Yes, I guessed that when you asked me to marry you." I could feel him blushing all the way across the ocean.

Exploring myself through dance allowed me to practice balancing between leading and following, as well as how to successfully enter into a partnership in a graceful, playful way. And so it was through dance that I started to venture into the world of dating again.

I came to think of my dating experiences as "stepping stones." Deep inside, I knew that I was not ready for a serious relationship. I was still in the process of exploring what I wanted in a romantic partnership. As I started to date, I learned about myself by seeing it in others. I started to see that this self-insight was the gift of a relationship.

At first, I thought that I would just skip all the stepping stone dates and wait until I was ready for the "real thing." But then I realized that the practice of dating was helping me to experience, explore, and understand how I wanted to feel in an intimate partnership. This exploration would tell me what kind of relationship would work. Every dating experience was meaningful and valuable no matter how involved it became or how long it lasted, because each was an important lesson in exploring myself. Each man I met mirrored where I was on my personal journey.

Dating became a journey of opening up my heart even further. I was being given the opportunity to feel more and think less. My heart was definitely breaking open as I practiced becoming emotionally available and vulnerable in a relationship—something many of us need after closing down our hearts to protect ourselves from the pains of a difficult partnership.

Perhaps most importantly, dating gave me the opportunity to practice using the knowledge of male and female energy present within us and within a relationship. I had been studying this for years, and would go on to teach and write about it later.

As I experienced the interactions of each romantic connection, I began to understand how much freedom I needed to allow myself in a partnership. Having been on my own for a while, I had the desire to be in an intimate relationship, but it was going to take some adjustments. As I was pondering all this one night, I channeled a poem:

The Woman That I Am

I am the wind. Do not try to hold onto me or place me in a container for you will only become frustrated.

Instead enjoy the pleasure as I whirl around you, caress your cheek with my touch, toss your hair, allowing it to release from its normal pattern.

Notice the way that I cause a stir all around you, sending things into a different order than would ordinarily occur.

Feel the freshness and the excitement of experiencing the energy around you as it dances with its own mind.

Breathe deeply and relax as I wind myself around you gently this way and that. Linger in this feeling and soak its kiss in.

Know that I can be hardly moving or racing at hurricane speed. It is all me and my strength is always a part of me.

Understand that I am always beside you, with you, ready for you to acknowledge me.

See the invisible for it is very real.

This poem just came out of me. It is a description of me, and how I feel as a woman. In parallel to this, it is how I feel Spirit, as a dancer always inside of you, invisible, but present. You cannot hold it tightly or it will slip away, just like a tango partner. This poem helped me understand how important it is to not possess your mate.

I realized I needed to look for a partner who could appreciate me for who I was at a very deep level, and then grant me the freedom to be myself. Likewise, the partner would allow me to do the same: see their pieces and accept them unconditionally for who they are. I looked forward to taking this lesson into future relationships and letting my partner enjoy being himself on his journey beside me.

After grounding my physicality with the exploration of dance, the new experience of various relationships rounded out my self-knowledge on a spiritual level. Through both, I learned how important it is to not take what others do personally and to give ourselves the love and nurturing we desire and deserve. When we practice these principles, we see our world shift, letting that which does not serve our higher good to fall away, while we fill ourselves with those that love and respect us.

Until we love, honor, and value ourselves, and until we learn to create healthy boundaries with others, we will not receive the same from our relationships. I discovered this in tango and in love.

Developing into my new life in Hawaii, I studied the meaning of "Aloha" and came to understand it has the same vibration as "Love." Love was becoming my base, my center, my thought, and my vision.

Shine Your Light

Nine

Becoming Angela

REMEMBER YOUR ROOTS;

SPREAD YOUR WINGS;

FIND YOUR PASSION;

LOVE LIFE;

ALWAYS REMEMBER WHO YOU ARE;

LET YOUR LIGHT SHINE.

—INSPIRATIONAL NOTE TO MY DAUGHTER, 2009

When my oldest daughter Sophia graduated from high school, I made a photo collage of her achievements for the graduation ceremony. The poem excerpt above is the inspirational words that came through me to share with her on the collage. I carried a copy of this poem with me during my period of self-discovery. This is now a core message I will share in my role as a teacher.

As I was finding myself, I started to understand the power

that words played in my life. I found that words could be a useful tool to help us connect to the meaning of our experiences. "A pearl is created from a grain of sand by an oyster through a process of irritation," was a phrase that seemed to hold special meaning for me at this point on my journey. C.G. Jung's words pair nicely with the pearl metaphor: "Life really does begin at forty. Up until then, you are just doing research."

I had done a lot of research, which was the friction, frustration, and discomfort of all the situations that had formed and refined me over the past several years. All this "stuff" I was going through had been polishing my soul. My divorce and evolving relationships with my children, as well as the exploration of my new self through dance and dating—it was all helping to craft a new me. But I wasn't quite finished; there were still unrefined and undiscovered pieces of my soul that needed polishing.

I still had to find all my pieces, and so I asked anyone and everything to show me my stuff. I wanted to learn how to see it in astrology charts, relationships, physical ailments, tarot cards, palm reading, numerology, and even in my toes (yes, there are actually toe readers, much like palm readers). I pursued any possibility outside of myself that might point to my inner manifestation.

After settling down in Hawaii, I almost immediately met a friend who recommended a teacher of lomilomi, an ancient Hawaiian form of massage and healing arts. I knew lomilomi had deep spiritual roots in ancient wisdom, but I had not yet explored it, so I eagerly signed up for a weekend workshop.

On the first day of class, our teacher Mary greeted us with a warm and open heart. Most of the participants in this small class were "locals," as they say in Hawaii. Some were native Hawaiian, some were Asian, but they were all mostly born and raised on the islands. They were curious how I had found my way into this group without having been on the island for very long. I began to tell my story, as I had grown used to doing regularly. Accepted for the time being, I sensed they continued to wonder what my journey was all about.

One weekend workshop turned into another and then another, and I soon found myself surrounded and accepted by my new "rainbow brothers and sisters," even though I stood out as the tall blond, freckled, white-skinned woman from the mainland. Although I had always understood that connecting with others had nothing to do with the color of our skin, the size of our bank accounts, or our native language, it was completely different experiencing this first hand. It was refreshing to feel so at home in this community, even though I rarely recognized what they ate, let alone said.

Many of the people who found this group felt that we were all being brought together for a reason. For those that believe in past lives, it is a common understanding that we are reunited with souls from different lifetimes for one specific reason or another.

Sometimes it is to play out themes in our soul's learning that we perhaps did not choose to play out in past lives. At other times, it is a group of souls being brought back together to draw on the strengths of their prior connections in order to expand their energies in this lifetime for the benefit of all.

Many in this group found our connection in the ancient Lemurian energy that Hawaii hosts, and which has played a major part in my transformation. As part of this connection, many of our workshops, get-togethers, and spiritual outings were designed to explore the ancient sacred sites of Oahu. It was on one such outing that I had one of my most significant experiences with my rainbow brothers and sisters.

There is a sacred spot, not far from the Makapu'u Heiau, that most Hawaiian healers know as the "Healings Pools." A heiau is an ancient Hawaiian place of worship and ceremony, still respected and vigilantly protected by the Hawaiians today. Led by Mary, we met there for a ceremony of chanting and celebration and to connect to the powerful energy that emanates from the pools.

We ventured from the beach onto the rocky point that thrusts into the ocean. Sharp volcanic rock dug into our feet as the open wind of the ocean pulled at our clothes. As Mary shared a story with the group, I found myself drifting off into a connection with an unseen force that seemed to welcome me into its arms. I stood open to the strong energy, arms extended down and out, with my palms open to the wind. I felt all the barriers inside of me slip first off of my shoulders, and then from around my heart and then, like a silk garment, the barriers gracefully fell to the jagged rocks below.

As my heart opened in that moment, tears silently slipped down my cheeks, slowly at first, and then like a river that I could not and did not want to stop. It was as if I finally gave myself permission to just let it all go, to let the tears flow until they could flow no more, to just allow myself to release the pain, the fear, and the struggle without any attachment, judgment, or shame. It was pain buried deep under a lifetime of experiences, and which had remained locked off from my conscious self, not yet ready to see my life from a new perspective. Off to my side, I felt the presence of my rainbow siblings, supportive but letting me have my own space.

When I spoke with Mary on the beach later, she looked knowingly at me and said, "You had quite a healing today." I smiled gently and nodded. I realized then that healing is something that happens when we are ready for it. By creating the environment for it to happen, we initiate it. A healer may be on your journey to provide the space and energy that invites and supports healing, but they do not heal you. That is your job, initiated by you and supported by the universe. The universe just waits for your readiness to let go of the pain, the anger, the fear, and all the negative energies related to these emotions that poisoned your body, fogged your mind, and weakened your spirit.

A Soul's Journey Home

Our group sat down on the beautiful, warm white sand to say a Hawaiian prayer to honor the ancestors. While we sat there I noticed small pieces of broken glass in the sand around me. As a man chanted with strength and power from the depth of his lungs, I started picking up all the glass pieces and holding them gently in the palm of my hand.

When the chant was over and there was a time for private reflection, I looked down and saw the handful of glass pieces. They were all different sizes and shapes, some brown, some green, but all were worn smooth by their time in the ocean. The movement of the tides and the sand had worn down their sharp edges. The tumbling of their journey had helped to soften the edges and buff them into pieces of prized art waiting to be found by a Hawaiian jeweler in search of new treasures.

I realized that I was holding the pieces of myself. I had found them and embraced them and felt the most beautiful calm I have ever known. Like me, like the sand in the oyster, the friction of their journey had polished them. After I reflected on our shared fate, I swung my hand and released them back into the ocean to be swept into the current, polished a little more, and then taken to the next place on their journey.

I gained an amazing sense of strength that day—a quiet strength, a peaceful strength. I was calm, content, and finally rid of all the pain I had held for so long. I gave thanks for all of the lessons I had gained through the exploration of my inner self and my various experiences. It had all paid off. I finally understood what the lessons had been trying to teach me. And in that moment, I was able to let it all go.

I enjoyed my time with the lomilomi group, and my rainbow brothers and sisters, but I knew that I would be expanding out from them eventually.

Mary had told me that my 'aumakua, the Hawaiian word for spirit animal, is the pueo, the native Hawaiian owl. Pueo also refers to a protector or guide—a soul that leads others through difficult times, connecting their physical and spiritual worlds. Mary told me she saw me doing wonderful things for many people, and I sensed that she saw the path that lay ahead of me. She told me that the tree that represented me was the pine. "Tall and strong, I reached straight for the heavens," she stated.

However, when the time came to give Hawaiian names to members of our group, I was a bit perplexed that I did not receive one from Mary. I asked another Hawaiian elder why I had not been given a name. She responded, "Do not be upset that you have not been given a name by Mary. I know that you know that a name is just a label, and I know that you know that you do not need a label to know who you are. Besides," she added, "It is not time yet. Be patient."

I went on to ask her why Susan, my other Hawaiian teacher, had not been more available to me now that I actually lived on-island. She replied, "She wants you to find your own way out of the forest. It is part of your learning and you are being tested."

Hawaii is not an easy place to integrate. As an outsider, it is hard to find a way into the community here. The saying goes: "The islands take you when they want you and they spit you out when they are done with you." You have to be here for a specific reason to succeed here, and you have to have an open heart to be accepted into the heart of the community. Even then, it is a test of your abilities and tenacity.

As I juggled the new energy of Hawaii, and embraced all of my newly refined pieces, my internal life found a new order. In response, everything in my outer world also began to shift quickly and positively.

I no longer needed the large family car, and the tiny condo full of someone else's belongings was not working for me either. With a friend's encouragement, I bought an "Angela car." My previous car had been purchased based on other people's needs, and now I needed a car for my new self, in my new island life. It was not selfish to buy the car that was right for me. Rather, I was honoring myself in the same way I would be inspiring others to honor themselves.

The discovery of my new condo is another story of manifesting what I wanted. For months I had been casually expressing the desire to find a place that had a view of the mountains. Often

I would say this, but then after a moment of silence, would mention how nice it would be to have a view of the ocean. There was no logic behind my seemingly contradictory desires—after all, you're either looking out to sea with the land behind you, or you're looking at the mountains with the ocean behind you. It's almost impossible to have the best of both worlds. I understood that, but still, it was a nice dream.

Nevertheless, the moment I walked into my current condo, I looked out the window to a stunning view of the mountains beyond the water of the bay. I knew that I had manifested into my life exactly what my soul had called for. I had sent out my intentions without trying to create the structure of how it would look, and I was ecstatic to have manifested my dreams so clearly. I now had a blueprint for manifestation that I knew I could reference whenever I needed to create. What's more, I could share this process with others.

Meanwhile, my house in Arizona had been up for sale for some time. I had decided after a couple of months in Hawaii that I would put my house up for sale when the kids told me that they preferred having just one home base at their dad's house. I found that they were enjoying spending time with me in Hawaii whenever their schedules allowed, rather than in our old home. We all seemed ready to move on from the old family home, and I trusted that what would happen with the house would be for the higher good of us all.

There had been no promising offers on the house as of yet. All I could do was wait as it sat on the market, suffering from the spiraling economy. Then, on my way to the airport for another visit to the children, my real estate agent called me.

"Hello, Angela!" my agent greeted me enthusiastically. "You have received an offer on your house that I think you will want to seriously consider. It's a bit low, but it is a cash deal and they want to close in a very short time frame." The timing was almost unbelievable, but I had enough experience at this point to recognize the signals of Spirit. I told her I was on my way to Scottsdale at that very moment, and we both shared a bellyful of laughter. It was time. I was ready to let go of all of the old trappings that no longer served me.

I was only in Scottsdale for two weeks, but we managed to strike a good deal with the prospective buyers. I would sell them the house in their narrow time frame, completely furnished, apart from a few pieces of the kids' furniture, my personal belongings, and selected kitchenware. In one fell swoop, I had let go of a home that I had known for ten years, as well as almost all of my possessions it contained. Things moved so quickly, it felt like the ground was shifting under my feet, but at the end of a frantic two weeks I had packed everything up and signed the appropriate contracts.

I was physically exhausted from lack of sleep, but at the same time I felt light, fresh, and free. The kids had adjusted to their dad's house as the base of operations, and it felt like we had successfully closed another chapter of our lives. Our home had served its function, and left us with special memories. Now it was time to go into the world as individuals, with our shared experiences to guide us. "Our home is wherever we are all brought together," I said, and the kids agreed. Home is not a physical place, it is the relationship that we have with each other, our connection from the heart.

With my personal business in order, I realized it was time to step into my role of pueo—a guide and teacher. I started my business of one-on-one coaching and immediately saw how comfortable I felt in this new role. I enjoyed trusting my abilities and sharing my insights and inspirations. I began to see the value of my work as others would tell me, "What you have shared with me is just what I needed to know at this time in my life, to help me shift into a higher level of being." It filled my soul to help other's realign with their true self and step into their power.

Soon, however, Spirit told me that I had to share my experience and journey with others in a larger way.

"Write. Tell your story," Spirit said again and again.

"But I am not a writer," I would respond.

"Yes, you are," Spirit said, "And don't allow yourself to be trained. If you do, then you will just have to unlearn the 'rules' to create in your way."

This was a true test of my faith in myself, to just embrace what I was inspired to do. And so, in my true Angela way, I began. With a leap of faith, I chose a workable first step. I started to convert my personal journal entries into blog posts, sharing my private thoughts, emotions, and experiences with the world. My blog, Shine-Your-Light.com was born, and my journey continued.

As I started to present myself to the world, I did not know what to call myself. By putting a label on myself, I felt I was limited to just one category. I constantly tried to define what it is that I do, realizing that as we continue to grow and expand, so will our work.

While I was in this phase of trying to find the words to describe what I do, I came across my neglected Hawaiian name book, buried under a stack of other books I used more frequently. Wondering why I was all of sudden being brought back into connection with this book, I flipped it open to the name "Angela." Short and simple, the Hawaiian equivalent of Angela is "Aulani," and the meaning was "messenger or sometimes angel." I now knew my Hawaiian name. I realized that someone does not have to give it to you—you will know it when it is time.

People ask me how long I have been doing the work that I do now. I tell them, "All my life, but now I charge money for it." Our gifts are always present. Sometimes we don't realize what they are, because they come so easily that we don't think they are a big deal. But our natural abilities are just waiting to be polished, like the grain of sand in the oyster, so that we can share them with others.

Shine Your Light

Ten

Around the World

"Chi ama, crede"
(He who loves, trusts)
—Traditional Italian Proverb

Having found my authentic self, I continued to follow the call of Spirit. Before long, my open heart and my implicit trust of Spirit led me to four continents in one year. It seemed natural, this geographical expansion—I had expanded internally, and now I just wanted to keep expanding out into the world.

Part of the call was my love of different cultures. I enjoy meeting authentic people in a foreign place, and seeing how they live their everyday lives. I had experience with the international dance community in Hawai'i, and also in Arizona, where I would mingle with different groups to find the new and unfamiliar in my own backyard.

Following Spirit, my travels taught me so much more about myself. I learned to trust myself in new circumstances, and gained the confidence of safety even when I was alone in strange places. Each new place I visited taught me lessons I will carry forever.

My journey to Australia began with a spontaneous call from Spirit. It was October 2010, and I was sitting on my lanai on Oahu, noticing the cooler, rainy weather blowing in as the season began to change. Not many realize there are actually subtle differences in the temperature and weather from season to season in Hawaii, and I knew it was going to become quite rainy this particular winter.

I laughed at myself as I thought, "I am living in paradise and I want it to be summer every day." In almost the same instant, I said to myself, "I want to go find summer!" I said it half in jest, but after that day, the idea of traveling to Australia continued to pop into my head.

I didn't fully understand this random attraction to Australia, so I investigated a little bit. I looked into the ancient history, wisdom, and culture of Australia and discussed it with colleagues. This exploration made the call too hard to ignore. I figured I was halfway there already—the middle of the Pacific Ocean—and so I took the plunge and bought an open-ended, one-way ticket to Sydney.

In mid-December, a few weeks before I was scheduled to leave, many friends voiced concern about my trip because of severe flooding in Australia. Three-quarters of the northeastern state of Queensland had been declared a disaster zone, and the torrential rain and rising rivers were displacing thousands of people. I didn't let the danger dissuade me. I knew that if I was meant to go there, I would, and the universe would keep me safe if it was meant to be. If not—well, so be it. I spent time with my children in Scottsdale over the holidays, and was on my way to Australia in the middle of January 2011.

I approached Australia with an open mind. I had no choice, because it was my first experience traveling out of the country by myself. I didn't know one person on the continent, and I didn't even have plans for where I would be staying after my first week.

I quickly discovered that Sydney was a very friendly city, and I had little reason to worry. The trickiest part was the Australian vocabulary and accent, which forced me to pay very close attention in conversations, even with native English speakers. In spite of my "translation" problem, I was well received by everyone I encountered. My enthusiasm helped a lot, and I often found people reciprocating my excitement. Even the concierges at my hotel found my enthusiasm contagious as they helped me look into the historic spiritual sites throughout the country.

Early on I took a bus tour from the center of the city to explore the natural wonders of the Blue Mountains on the edge of Sydney. I wanted to see how the countryside and Australian life outside of the city looked. I also imagined that I would be able to go on a nature hike, connecting directly to the land.

The witty bus driver resembled my stereotypical vision of a man from Down Under: sandy blond, athletic, with the rugged good looks of an outdoorsman. He was a fountain of facts and insights about Sydney, and continued to share his knowledge of the Australian countryside as we ventured into the Blue Mountains. However, the more he spoke, the more I understood that I would not be attempting any walkabout on my own in the back country of Australia.

The driver told a story of a hiker who had been stranded in the forest of the Blue Mountains for several days. The rescue team that found him could not believe the hiker had survived the deadly spiders and other dangerous creatures on the land. It would be unwise to risk walking through the brush by myself. Instead, I looked forward to what I would experience on this bus tour, enjoying the beautiful Australian scenery from the safety of a group with an experienced guide.

We stopped at a lookout of the Blue Mountains, where we could see the famously beautiful Three Sisters rock formation rising out of the vast forest. To my delight, we were soon led down a trail to explore the woods, which quickly engulfed us. My eyes, nose, and ears were filled with the sensations of this exotic and dangerously beautiful landscape. The flowers and trees, the animals and insects, everything was so unique and different from anything I had seen before. Even the wind that made the leaves at my feet dance, blew through my hair with a magic I'd never experienced. The only disappointment was the lack of kangaroos, which I had been hoping all day long to see hopping along the roadside.

On our return trip, I sat next to a young German woman who was traveling throughout Australia alone. She was a student on an extended vacation between her undergraduate and graduate programs, occasionally working to fund her travels. To save money, she often "couch surfed"—something I had never heard of.

CouchSurfing is an online organization that connects travelers around the world with local people who are willing to open their homes and offer a free couch to crash on for the night. It's a great opportunity to share cultures and to make friends all over the globe. I was intrigued by this brave young woman, and the notion of couch surfing.

I asked her many questions about her best and worst

experiences when couch surfing. It seemed like such a risky way to travel! Eventually I just blurted, "How do you do it?" She calmly replied, "It is about trust." I was astonished by the words that came out of her mouth, and sat there speechless. This message was filling every corner of my life. Her answer made me realize how simple trust can be, and yet I wondered why we make it so hard.

After a few days of exploring Sydney and the surrounding areas, I began to realize how large and spread out Australia is. It was dawning on me that the places I wanted to visit, such as Uluru—a remote sacred area still inhabited by the aboriginal people—really required additional air travel and more extensive planning. So I began to think of this trip as a nice introduction to Australia, and promised myself that I would return someday to get to know her and her people more thoroughly. It would be a wonderful adventure to share with my children in the future, and when we did, I would have a better idea of what to do.

One thing I did immerse myself in while staying in Sydney was the dance community. I was fortunate to meet some wonderful people who embraced my love of dance and life. Though I met interesting and generous people through dance, I felt the call to return to Scottsdale.

Little issues from home had been popping up here and there,

distracting me from Australia. I still had personal belongings in storage in Scottsdale, and since I had sold my home, I had to stay at a hotel or with a friend when I visited the children. I knew I would be spending a lot of time with my kids in between my international trips that year, and so I would need a small home base in Arizona. There was also the fact that I wasn't sure how long I would be in Hawaii, and I wanted a place to return to if my son needed to be with me while still in high school. In addition, I was anticipating spending more time on the mainland as my business expanded.

All these things were going through my head as I flew back to Hawaii. It was time to practice what I had learned, and so I started to manifest a new home in Scottsdale that would be just right for me. I pictured the place that I wanted, what it would look like, and what it would feel like. I let myself feel as if I were already there. Using my imagination and inner knowing, I sent my energy out to Spirit to help me create this new vision.

I explained my desires to my realtor in Scottsdale, describing the sort of condo that I wanted to have as my home base. I would have just two weeks on my next visit to find the perfect place. We exchanged a few emails and narrowed down a large list of properties to ten choices we would have time to check out when I was in town.

We looked at properties on one of those rare cold and rainy days in Scottsdale. The weather and the prospects for my new home were grim. Nothing appealed to me until we came to the last property on our list. Walking through the door, I immediately knew we had found the right place. The layout and energy was everything that I had projected for the universe to lead me to. We made an offer and closed the deal within 10 days—everyone involved in the transaction was amazed, saying they had never done a deal so fast. I was learning through experience that there is no reason that we cannot manifest what we want quickly.

After attending Samantha's high school, and Michael's middle school graduations, I was off to Italy. The plan was to meet up with Sophia, who was studying abroad for a semester. It was a time of exploration and growth for both of us, and I was happy to be with her on her journey as she, too, ventured farther out into the world.

Most of my time in Italy was spent in Florence, immersing myself in the culture, while taking daily excursions to the surrounding areas. The city life of Italy was more sensual than Australia, and I explored Florence by indulging in the exquisite cuisine and local sights. I spent hours in the cathedrals and art museums, absorbing the history of the people, which seemed to infuse even the cobblestones the modern Italians commuted over each day. The rich past that could be seen everywhere, paired with the lyrical Italian language I fumbled with, made Italy seem much more foreign than Australia. This made it an excellent opportunity to practice remaining confident in my authentic self while in a strange place.

I spent a long weekend with my daughter exploring the Cinque Terre region, the renowned coastline of picturesque and almost inaccessible terraced cities on the Italian Riviera. It was quite an adventure for my daughter and me, finding our way through these ancient streets that wound through the five main villages. Hiking the treacherous ridge trails that overlooked the sea hundreds of feet below, interpreting the train schedules, and tracking down the ferries that carried us from town to town was an educational adventure for both of us. We lived in the moment, and trusted that the universe would always provide the next step for us if we maintained our faith.

In Italy I gained the confidence to protect myself as a lone woman. One instance in particular affirmed my personal strength and power. It happened on one of my many train trips, as I sat by the window in a seating arrangement designed for four people: two pairs of seats facing each other. Two men suddenly joined me on the aisle seats facing each other. When the train conductor approached them for tickets, all he received was an intimidating glare and a grunt from one of the men, and he left quickly without seeing their stubs. The two large men sat with their knees touching, leaving no space for me to pass if I wanted to exit. Turning towards me, the man beside me silently projected an aggressive and intimidating energy and began to press his knee against mine, invading my space. I observed his actions, but did not retreat into fear. Instead, I projected light and a confidence in my safety all around me. As he sensed my strength, I stood, and pushing through the men's knees, walked fearlessly to the end of the cabin, making sure to not engage with his energy. If I had done so, I sensed he would have turned the encounter into a struggle or fight.

A month of navigating Italy and connecting with my daughter was very healing. It was a challenging practice of my newfound skill of living in the moment and following the signs of the universe. I can honestly say that I returned to Hawaii with more confidence in myself than I had ever known.

No sooner was I back in Hawaii than my dance teacher told me about his upcoming trip to Tokyo, Japan for a dance festival. He explained how the festival was a source of anticipated joy and excitement for the Japanese after a traumatic and emotional year in the wake of the earthquake and tsunami that had brought chaos and destruction to the Tokyo region. His eagerness inspired me, and I knew I was supposed to go as well—Spirit called me to do whatever work might present itself once I got to Japan.

With just a few weeks to prepare for the trip, I trusted Spirit to guide me in the hectic task of studying the maps, finding places to stay, and briefly acquainting myself with the rudiments of the Japanese language. As always, I just kept walking forward, knowing I would be supported.

Stepping off the plane at an airport outside of Tokyo, I immediately felt more foreign than I ever had before. The place was bustling with energy, and I stood out sharply in a crowd of mostly Asian people hurrying along with their lives. Once again, I observed the feelings that came from being in a place where I could not blend in with the crowd.

With no grasp of the written or spoken language, I was immediately lost as I exited the subway into the bustling streets of Tokyo. Fortunately, the Japanese people are extremely gracious, and did their best to give me directions, though all the while warning me that the district where I was staying (Asakusa) was going to be a zoo—it was National Heritage Day, and the festivities would be in full swing in the area of my hotel. Before long, a charming old man guided me directly to my building, and left me with a welcoming blessing. All around me the celebration of Japan's ancient culture surged with a stunning display of colors and music and smiling faces. I felt it was auspicious for me to have arrived on such an important and special day.

Though I had considered the possibility of arranging a healing workshop while in Tokyo, I ended up just following the lead of Spirit, exploring the holy places of Japan. The highlight of my trip was my journey to Kyoto, the old imperial capital of Japan, an area steeped in ancient history and full of sacred temples.

It was fascinating to be in an ancient spiritual city of the East, after having so recently explored ancient spiritual cities of the West. In Australia, the spiritual traditions seemed almost forgotten by the people I met in Sydney, though they still had much respect for the natural wonders of the land. In Italy, life was lived in such close proximity to their heritage that the traditions, while respected, were almost taken for granted. In Kyoto, there were more Japanese appreciating the sacred temples and grounds than there were foreign tourists. Visitors from all over the country filled the streets to capture the beauty of the temples amidst the stunning colors of the autumn foliage. The energy of the people, the temples, and the forest surrounding the area was loving and peaceful and full of gratitude. In the end, I saw how similar all humanity is when it comes to treasuring our past, in spite of our different languages and spiritual philosophy.

My last day in Kyoto was a busy one, traveling by train to the surrounding areas to visit three specific cities and their attractions. First, I hurried through the amazing forest of red gates at the Temple of a Thousand Doorways in Fushimi-ku.

Next, it was on to Uji, which was beautiful, but I was in a hurry to get to Nara. I managed to make it back to the station just in time to catch one of the last trains.

As I waited for the train to Nara, I meditated on the energies of the places I had just seen, and found myself wondering about Spirit's path for me. I had been told that I was going to meet a man while traveling in Japan who would share ancient knowledge with me. I had not yet encountered this man, but I remained open and observant, certain that he would cross my path. As I pondered this, an older man sat next to me on the bench to wait for the train.

It is not typical in Japanese culture for a strange man to converse with a foreign woman, especially for the older generations who still strictly adhere to the formal traditions. And yet before I knew it, this gentleman was opening up to me about his travels. When he found that I was on the same journey as he—exploring the temples of the area—he became even more excited and friendly. He shared some ancient writings he had been reading, emphasizing one phrase in particular: Ichi-go ichi-e literally, "one time, one meeting." He looked into my eyes and said, "This meeting between you and I was supposed to happen. You should not miss your chance when things are presented to you." Clearly, Spirit was speaking through him.

I enjoyed our brief friendship on the train ride to Nara, but as we disembarked, he said, "Follow me and I will lead you. I don't think you will be able to make it to all the places you want to go." With that, he started walking very fast, weaving through the streets of the city. I couldn't keep up and soon had to stop to use the restroom. When I reemerged onto the street, I figured that our paths had parted, only to find him pop back up in front of me. "You're never going to make it at this rate!" he declared enthusiastically, and in spite of my protests, insisted on leading me on a private tour of Nara at a breakneck pace.

It was an amazing experience. Before long we were admiring the stunning three-story pagoda of Kōfuku-ji. He snapped a picture of me as the sun began to descend behind the pagoda and then it was off to Tōdai-ji. This world-famous temple called to my energy so intimately that I felt I had been there in a previous life. The gratitude I felt for this man who had led me through Nara mixed powerfully with the sensations of this ancient place, and I found myself again and again stopped in my tracks as I grappled with an onslaught of emotions.

At Tōdai-ji, sika deer, considered by Shintoism to be heavenly messengers, wander the grounds of the temple freely. They interact peacefully with the visitors on the streets and lawns, not at all afraid of humans. I stood in the gentle misty rain falling from the heavens as a lone deer came and greeted me with tender kindness. I felt at peace, knowing I had accomplished what I was meant to in Japan. Now I could go home.

Traveling around Japan, I was inspired by the gratitude and kindness of the people. Seeing foreigners cheered the Japanese people. They found hope and confidence in meeting people brave enough to visit their country even after the horrible disaster that had torn apart their lives. They expressed genuine appreciation for my visit almost every day. They seemed to gain courage to face their circumstances with the knowledge that people from around the world cared for them. I felt that I had made a difference all by myself, touching people's lives in a way that mattered. Following Spirit, I learned that one person could make a difference. Most of all, I couldn't wait to share my foreign experiences with my children.

My relationship with my children was perhaps the most important development during nearly a year of traveling around the world. By exploring my new self in foreign situations, I was able to work through the guilt of the choice I had made of not living with the kids full time. I may have traveled to countries all over the globe, but it was the time I spent with my children, whether in Italy, or back in Scottsdale, that meant the most to me.

When we reconnected between my overseas trips, I shared

stories and pictures of the foreign lands I had visited, and they shared their life adventures I had missed. I could sense the excitement they felt as I shared my new wisdom of the world and of myself, and I was thrilled to hear their stories of learning and growth. I could sense their strength and confidence growing stronger. I had given myself permission to expand into the world, and as a result, I saw my choice had allowed us all to expand in ways I could never have imagined.

I had always hoped my children would understand that they were citizens of the world, and now I was showing them how to be one. I could see the excitement build as we discussed our dreams of future adventures. Sophia's experiences of a semester in Italy stimulated our imagination of living in foreign places. For all of us, the world had become an intriguing place to explore, and its people were friends that we had yet to meet.

My children displayed their courage and intelligence that year, revealing to me how well prepared they were for a life of independence. Of course, Sophia was well on her way with a new life at college, and demonstrated her power during our travels in Italy. With Samantha, the moment of realization came before I traveled to Italy during the celebrations of her high school graduation.

Her school ceremony was moving, but it was the Senior

Recognition Celebration of the mother-daughter National Charity League that really opened my eyes. She had developed with this philanthropy group for six years, and now, as a graduating senior, she and her peers were given the opportunity to share their experiences with a large crowd of mothers, daughters, and extended family. When my daughter's turn on the stage came, I could see she was terrified, but with a good friend standing behind her in support, she began her speech.

"The first thing that I want to thank my mother for, is her emotions that she has shared with me." The tears immediately began to flow, and for a few moments she couldn't continue. As she stood there in her rawness, I sat in the audience sending her strength, anxious to see what she would be sharing with the room of friends and acquaintances that surrounded us.

She mustered her courage, found her center, and continued to talk about the things she had gone through for the last couple years. She talked about the shock of experiencing things that she had only thought about as problems in other people's lives. But she concluded on a positive note, speaking about the confidence she had gained in herself through her trials. She knew she would be fine continuing onto college and leading a healthy life on her own. Her mix of pain and joy was tangible to everyone in the room, and in that moment, I witnessed her turn the corner from a confused and hurt girl, to an empowered young woman.

Michael was also stepping into his own. Having trained hard, he was prepared to enter high school and the basketball team, all the while remaining a beautifully gentle soul. During one of our well-loved dinner dates, I realized that he was enjoying blossoming into a closer relationship with his father. Soon, his last sister would be leaving for college, and he would have even more male bonding time.

That year it felt as if my children and I had climbed to the top of a new mountain. The journey had been long and hard, and many times the path forward had been almost invisible. But now we had reached the summit and had a chance to catch our breaths and look around at the glorious view of new beginnings that surrounded us.

Shine Your Light

Eleven

Home

"WE ARE ALL VISITORS TO THIS TIME, THIS PLACE.
WE ARE JUST PASSING THROUGH.
OUR PURPOSE HERE IS TO OBSERVE, TO LEARN, TO
GROW, TO LOVE...AND THEN WE RETURN HOME."
—AUSTRALIAN ABORIGINAL PROVERB

I have found my passion. I have found myself and it is there that I live. It comes from the center of my heart, and all that I do is touched by it. It is a space of contentment that is hard to even begin to explain. It is home. All else are details waiting to be "in-joyed."

There is a quote of uncertain origin, often attributed to James Michener, but possibly originating from Unitarian minister L.P. Jacks. Whoever said it, I think it can help express what I am saying:

"The master in the art of living makes little distinction between his work and his play, his labor and his leisure, his mind and his body, his education and his recreation, his love and his religion. He hardly knows which is which. He simply pursues his vision of excellence at whatever he does, leaving others to decide whether he is working or playing. To him he's always doing both."

Everyone's real job in life is the discovery of his or her true self. This alone leads us to wholeness and happiness. When we stay on the true path to ourselves, both leisure time and labor become opportunities to enjoy our lives and to learn.

I also agree with Herman Hesse who said, "The true profession of man is to find his way to himself." Hesse was repeating what humanity has known for many ages. The ancient Greeks founded some of their greatest philosophy on this same dictum: "Know Thyself." Working towards self-knowledge is the greatest work we can do in our lives, affecting more than we can even comprehend. Working on healing and finding our true self—the divine within—is the way to create a world of love and light. By starting at the individual level, we can affect the universal level.

As I write this chapter, I am sitting in my heaven on earth. The sky is full of graceful clouds constantly changing form over the top of the mountains, while the reflection of the sun on the bay dances with vivacity in a million sparkling lights. The various birds of the island serenade me, sharing their freedom, each with a unique song. In the distance, a car passes, a dog barks, and a girl's laughter echoes down the street. All is at peace with itself in a gentle, flowing calmness. It reflects my own mood as I sit here, grateful and inspired.

Of course, there is always a dark side to our journey, and pain is a necessary part of our development. The secret is learning the alchemy of turning pain into compassion, and fear into love.

I have been transformed by all the heartache I have endured. At one point, my heart felt like a raw mess that I held exposed in my very hands—stripped, bruised, and aching, it felt as if I held the heartache of the entire world. And yet I found this pain to be a gift, an opportunity to love at a deeper level than I imagined possible. It was a gift to be able to see the beauty in our struggles, and the chance to discover newfound love of myself, of others, and of life itself.

We must learn to embrace these opportunities in a state of joy. No direction or choice is wrong if it is taken with passion and faith. And so, to this day, I live my life with passion, in the moment, following my heart with all my joy.

Now that I am at peace with who I am and how I live, I have fully stepped into my role as an inspirational teacher. Men and women come to me looking for the peace that I speak of and personally know. Nearly every one of these encounters is a chance to educate others about the possibilities that hide in the difficult moments of our lives.

One of the biggest hurdles during these transitions is to understand the significance of what is happening to us. Often, things do not become clear until later, when what seemed like separate pieces all come together to reveal the full picture of our soul. I experienced this when I received the message from Spirit of my bird nature, before I ever considered moving to Hawaii. In the moment, I was grateful for the beauty of the message, but now I see the depth of this message in a whole new way.

When coaching clients through difficult transitions, I often find myself saying, "Remember that in this transition you are in a beautiful place. You've been knocked momentarily off your track, and now you're just sitting here on your butt. This is the perfect moment to just sit with yourself and honor that place where you have fallen off. This is an opportunity to fall out of the rat race, to fall away from your old patterns and to become the observer." Approximately 95% of behavior is subconscious programming. Our work is to become conscious. There is nothing like a jarring bump from your journey to awaken that consciousness. The universe designs the experiences you are going through with good intentions: to become conscious of yourself. When you embrace this knowledge, you will respond to difficulties in a new way. You will stop reacting without thought, and you will become able to avoid the triggers that previously tripped you up.

When I tell people of my own journey and new consciousness, of my triggers and traps, a common response is, "You're brave. You are so brave."

I don't shy away from the compliment. "Yes," I say, "Yes I am. It took a lot of courage." Living freedom does take courage. It took courage to know I was not avoiding my responsibilities to my family, but actually following the true path of my soul. It always takes courage to embrace the unknown and to accept our inability to answer every question, whether they come from inside or from others.

Living freedom remains a constant challenge. Recently, I was talking with a friend of mine about the relationship that we both knew I was ready for and wanted to manifest. We laughed together at the joy of feeling the certainty of Spirit, and our readiness to embrace a new beginning. It was exhilarating, but still there had been no manifestation of my desire.

My friend gave me a wonderful gift in that moment. She suggested that I write down a list of everything that I am now. The list should represent all the things that I truly am and that I love doing. "Keep it on the refrigerator," she suggested, "or a place where you can always see it. This list will be a constant reminder to keep those parts and passions alive as you are drawn into a new world. It will keep you from accidentally surrendering too much of yourself, and to maintain the person your future partner will fall in love with. Otherwise, if you change, your fire may die."

I keep that list with me to this day, and give my clients the same advice. With faith in Spirit, life will be a success, so long as you remember to not walk away from your list. Always remember who you are, and keep those pieces alive.

I have since met a wonderful man who reflects my unconditional love and visions. I do not know where this relationship will lead me, but I am not impatient. I am simply open, ready, and living in the moment. I know my path will unfold naturally to continue to support my growth and to match my energy. There is no rush, for I have achieved so much in so little time. I sold my home, gave away most of my belongings, and traveled the world inspiring others. Mutual healings have taken place, messages of Spirit have been exchanged, and connections of love and light have united me with a myriad of souls.

I have found my pieces, but look forward to endless growth. I cannot wait for new exploration, experiences, and lessons that will inevitably come as I live a full life in my new awareness. I look forward to all that I will teach, and all that I will learn from those who come to me for guidance. I am continually learning more from those souls most precious to me, my children.

My oldest daughter is now the president of her sorority. I visited her not long ago on a "Moms' Weekend" hosted by her sorority. While I enjoyed catching up with her, I was overwhelmed by the flurry of activities that surrounded us. She seemed perfectly comfortable letting the other young ladies run the functions of the busy weekend, and rarely interfered. I was a little puzzled, since she was the president, and I asked her about not being more involved in the process. She smiled at me. "Mom—I am empowering them." She was learning, as I had, to trust and allow others to find their own power.

You may remember that my journey through the tunnel began with numerology and astrology. My sun sign is Taurus, represented by the planet Venus. For the last eight years, Venus has been going through what is known in astrology as "The Venus Transit." This rare event occurs when Venus eclipses the sun at the beginning and end of this astrological period. In this case, it occurred in June of 2004 and 2012. When Venus, the planet of relationships, eclipses the Sun, the dark side of humanity is brought into focus. It is clear to me now that as a Taurus, my transformation mirrored this passage of Venus very closely. Beyond my own life, the Venus Transit has been a collective journey for humanity.

If you have found yourself, as I have, in a time of transition, stop and reflect on what has occurred. Can you hear the call of Spirit leading you to the pieces of yourself you have been ignoring? Now is the opportunity to embrace them and to lead a new life.

Within each of us is a story waiting to unfold. It is the story of us stepping back into our power and aligning with our authentic self. It is the story of us overcoming our fears that we do not have the ability or resources to stand on our own in our truth. The details of your story may be different than mine, but if you believe in abundance and your ability to create a life that supports you, you will find that you have more power to create than you ever imagined. You already have everything that you need. The biggest step is remembering and trusting that you have it.

In the spring of 2012, I knew my new destiny was to lead and teach by example. But still I struggled. Spirit would have none of my excuses, and kept insisting that I write my story. The more I protested that I was not a writer, the more Spirit encouraged me. Spirit said, "Write what comes to you intuitively. Tell your story. There will come a day when all you do is write."

And here I am. Writing the book that Spirit has told me for years I would create. I hope you have gained some insight from my story. But remember, there will always be more to discover and learn. I am already working on a book about the purpose and meaning of relationships, something that is relevant to all of us. I leave you with a final poem I recently wrote. Thank you for taking this journey with me.

Love Is

Love is not a place outside of you…it is an essence
within you from which all else comes.

Love is not something that you can hold onto…it is
something to be experienced and enjoyed.

Love is not something that you can buy…it is free
and expands the more you embrace it.

Love is not something that you can own…it
cannot be contained.

Love does not ever leave you…you carry it within you
forever.

Love is not a person…it is a reflection of you witnessed
in another.

Love is not a time...it is timeless and can be tapped into whenever you like.

Love cannot be taken away from you...it is yours always to be felt.

Love is not illusive...it is as close as your next breath.

Love is not something that chooses you...you choose it whenever you desire.

Love is not something that you need to acquire...it is within you waiting to be embraced and expressed.

Love is not a mystery...it is the core of who you are.

Sources

Chiles, William 'Pila'. The Secrets and Mysteries of Hawaii: A Call to the Soul. Deerfield Beach, Fla.: Health Communications, 1995.

Goodwin, Matthew Oliver. Numerology: The Complete Guide. Franklin Lakes, NJ: The Career Press, 1981.

Hamaker-Zondag, Karen. The Yod Book: Including a Complete Discussion of Unaspected Planets. York Beach, ME: Samuel Weiser, 2000.

Hay, Louise L. Heal Your Body. Exp. Rev. Ed. Carlsbad, CA: Hay House, 2005.

Jaffe, Kabir, and Ritama Davidson. Indigo Adults: Forerunners of the New Civilization. Lincoln, NE: iUniverse, 2005.

Karén, Michelle. Astrology for Enlightenment. New York, NY: Atria Books, 2008.

Lass, Martin. Chiron: Healing Body & Soul. Woodbury, MN: Llewellyn Publications, 2005.

Root, Eileen M. Hawaiian Names English Names. Booklines Hawaii, 1987.

Sams, Jamie, and David Carson. Medicine Cards: The Discovery of Power Through the Way of Animals. Rev. Exp. Ed. New York, NY: St. Martin's Press, 1999.

Spiller, Jan. Astrology for the Soul. New York, NY: Bantam Dell, 2008.

Williamson, Marianne. The Age of Miracles: Embracing the New Midlife. 2nd Ed. U.S.A.: Hay House, 2008.

Woolfolk, Joanna Martine. The Only Astrology Book You'll Ever Need. Twenty-First Century Ed. Lanham, MD: Taylor Trade Publishing, 2006.

www.shine-your-light.com

www.ingramcontent.com/pod-product-compliance
Lightning Source LLC
Chambersburg PA
CBHW021145090426
42740CB00008B/949